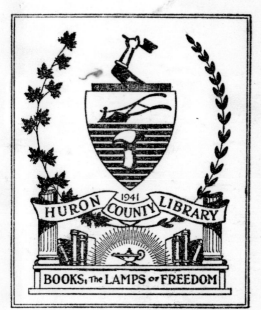

1941

HURON COUNTY LIBRARY

BOOKS, The LAMPS of FREEDOM

SIKANASKA TRAIL

By J. S. Gowland

SMOKE OVER SIKANASKA

SIKANASKA TRAIL

By

J. S. Gowland

Illustrated by
Christopher Brooker

London
WERNER LAURIE

First published in 1956
by T Werner Laurie Limited
1 Doughty Street London WC1
Printed in Great Britain
by the Surrey Fine Art Press Ltd
London and Redhill

R 8129

CONTENTS

To my son, Kenyon,

SGT. PILOT K. S. GOWLAND, R.A.F.,

killed in action on the night of

5/6 November 1940 at Ootmarsum, Holland.

PREFACE

MY ADVENTURES as a Forest Ranger, described in my book *Smoke Over Sikanaska,* proved sufficiently interesting to cause numerous readers to urge me to write a sequel. This book is the result, though it would be inaccurate to describe it as a sequel. The work, in fact, which contains the high lights of experiences which happened at various times, is more a contemporary of the first book than an account of subsequent happenings.

The book is not limited to my own experiences, although they naturally form the bulk and basis of the material. Included, also, are the experiences of others which are worthy of record because they reveal the true spirit and background of Canada, and because of their intrinsic interest. Although fictitious names are used, all persons referred to are, or were, as real as Wind Lake itself and the Rocky Mountains in which it is situated.

The background is the same as that found in the previous book, there is no reiteration of any of the incidents recorded in *Smoke Over Sikanaska,* but several of the characters appearing in that book, as well as many new ones, have a place in this second volume.

This, then, is the book I have written for those who so liked *Smoke Over Sikanaska* that they requested a second of the same kind. If they enjoy this as much as they assured me they enjoyed the first, then the writing of the second will have been more than worth while.

J. S. GOWLAND

1956

I : TRAIL CLEARING

THE FIRST DAY of May was, for me, one of keen expectancy and excitement. For this was the day on which I left my ranch and set out for the Rockies, returning to the mountains which had won my heart.

Originally economic need had driven me to take up the work of a Forest Ranger. My Canadian ranch was a small one; too small to keep me during the depressed thirties, and the six months' work in the mountains supplemented my far from adequate income. A single summer in the Rockies, however, alone and at nine thousand feet, had been sufficient to inspire in me such a love of the mountains that wages were of the least consideration. The life so thrilled and satisfied me that I would have spent the summer there for nothing more than my keep.

The soaring, awe-inspiring peaks, the valleys clothed with stands of pine and spruce, and seamed with glittering creeks almost overcrowded with trout; the smooth-surfaced lakes which presented an inverted picture of the unrivalled landscape, and the wild creatures, ranging from jack rabbits to grizzly bears, made up a world of immeasurable interest and delight.

There was the solitude, too, and the freedom, and the

11

satisfying feeling that the vast region formed a kingdom
for which I was responsible.

Having arranged with a neighbour to keep an eye on
my cattle, and with everything I needed packed ready
for an early start, I greeted the first of May with a happy
sense of anticipation. The first stretch of the journey lay
over the eighty miles to the Ranger Station at Colston,
where I was to meet Pete McLean, the Chief Ranger of
the area in which my district lay. By horse it was a two
day trip if the going proved easy, but a third day would
be needed if conditions were against me.

My horses were groomed and fed, and I felt certain
they knew where they were going. Three in number,
they were excellent companions, although they lacked
nothing in variety. "Paint" was a "blue" and white
paint horse or pinto, a good-looking mare with a definite
Arab strain, and she served as my main saddle horse.
"Barney," whom I also rode on occasion, was a large and
rather ungainly gelding. Despite the fact that his appearance was against him, he was the fastest walker I have
ever seen, and his powers of endurance were remarkable.
On one occasion he carried me seventy miles in little
more than twelve hours, reaching his destination in far
better condition than his rider.

"Lady," the third horse in my string, was a chestnut
mare of matronly proportions and manner, who could
carry three hundred pounds over rough and precipitous
trails without so much as twitching an ear.

Astride Paint, and with Barney and Lady carrying my
belongings, I set out, heading west. The first day passed
uneventfully, ending when I reached an Indian encampment, where I stayed for the night. Many of the Indians
were known to me, and we exchanged our news before
settling in our tents.

The following day I was soon traversing the main highway, the least pleasant part of the journey; for the day
was hot, the road dusty and seemingly endless, and was
frequented by cars which flashed by, leaving behind
them spreading plumes of grit and acrid gasoline fumes.

It was a relief when Colston at last edged into view, and I took to the short trail which freed me from the highway and led to the Ranger Station on the edge of the town. It lay beneath one of the great mountain ranges that hemmed the valley on either side, and was the range beyond which, to the south, my district lay.

Turning my horses into the pasture, I went to join Pete McLean and his wife, and to receive instructions concerning the work of the summer. After a meal, I visited the store in the mining town of Colston to make some last minute purchases, and particularly to buy oats for my horses. It was too early for the feed higher up to satisfy them, and I always had a few oats with me to keep them contented. Not that they were fractious or troublesome. They never strayed, and they never hit the back trail as soon as they were loose, a habit indulged by most horses, and one which causes plenty of inconvenience. Nor was it necessary to hobble them. Paint never wandered far, and as Barney and Lady kept close to her, the three were always on hand together. Because Barney and Lady followed Paint so faithfully it was never necessary to lead them when carrying packs. They simply followed their leader, and were generally close on her heels.

The next morning was warm, and with a sparkle in the air. As I packed my horses I looked up towards Indian Pass, thousands of feet above, and beyond which lay the district for which I was responsible. There was no snow in the valley, but I could see that there was plenty of it higher up. At this time of the year the pass always had its full share, and only a short time before it would have prevented any attempt to break through. Efforts to negotiate Indian Pass in winter are highly dangerous, although foolhardy individuals have chanced their luck from time to time, some paying for their temerity with their lives.

But this was May, and spring had advanced to the stage where there was no sign of dangerous masses of snow overhanging the pass. Pete McLean, too, was reassuring. He had been to the summit to fix the telephone lines, and he said that the pass looked safe enough. As it satisfied his experienced eye, I set out with plenty of confidence.

The trail to the pass presented no difficulties for the first couple of miles, but beyond the timberline it was exceedingly steep. In some places it was almost sheer, footholds being provided by nothing more than a series of rocky steps over which cascaded water from the melting snow.

The horses, out of condition after long winter months of little or nothing to do, found the going tested them severely, and they were soon soaked with sweat. Later in the season, although it would be much hotter, they would take such a journey in their stride, but they were in no state to do so then, and I rested them frequently. I also dismounted, leading Paint until the pass was reached, for there the way was level and called for less exertion. But the trail was narrow and cut into the steep mountain side, and it was covered with snow to a depth of three or four feet.

At this altitude the air remained chill, and the snow was still firm. Thus there was little danger of a slide, but the surface was crusty and we had to plough through it. The trail, of course, was hidden, and we were negotiating nothing more than a very steep slope of unbroken snow. Knowing Paint's good sense, and also knowing that she was as sure footed as a goat, I left things to her. She snorted in disgust and pawed at the snow to make sure of her ground, and she had some difficulty in breaking the trail as it was nearly breast high. Had I tried to make my way through on foot I should have floundered hopelessly, probably lost the trail, and had Paint stepping on my heels.

There were only a few hundred yards of this before the trail dipped into the valley beyond. I was about half way through the stretch of snow, and feeling that the worst lay behind, when a commotion in my rear caused me to look round anxiously. There, several yards down the slope, was Lady, her legs sticking uphill, a pile of

snow she had pushed ahead of her preventing her from sliding farther. Luckily there had been no need to tie the horses head to tail or we should all have been down and in very much of a tangle. Luckily, too, Lady made no attempt to rescue herself from her undignified and uncomfortable position. She lay on her side, the weight of her pack downhill, her legs up, so that she was almost upside down. No doubt she felt too helpless to do anything to help herself, and I prayed that she would continue to feel that way. For if she started to struggle there was grave risk that she would start a real slide, and that would have proved disastrous.

I scrambled off Paint, leaving her lines trailing on the snow, knowing she would stay anchored by them as she had been trained to do. Then, with Barney content to stand and doze, I scrambled down to Lady. This was no picnic, for the snow was deep enough to prevent me pushing my way through, but it was not firm enough to form any support. Reaching her, I set about getting her pack off as quickly as possible. Fortunately, she was on her right side, which allowed me to get at the final knot of the diamond hitch. But I had to burrow in the snow extensively before I eventually freed her of her heavy pack boxes. Her top pack, which consisted of a gross of eggs, half a sack of oats and my sleeping bag, I wedged in the snow to prevent them slipping farther down the slope. But I placed it well away from her, knowing that in her efforts to regain her feet she would stamp all over, playing havoc with my gross of eggs.

There was a great depth of snow filling the bottom of the ravine and it was more than likely that it was not solid. There could be large hollow places beneath the surface into which one could fall, to be buried by the tons of snow which would follow one down.

Climbing above Lady as far as the halter shank would allow, I pulled and coaxed, employing the appropriate noises of encouragement to get the mare back on her feet. For a time, however, she was much too frightened to so much as move. At last she scrambled up with a prodigious heave. But the slope was so steep that she was scrambling frantically to secure a footing. She regained the trail, but in such terrified haste that she knocked me flying, as I was so hampered by snow that I had no chance to jump out of her way.

It took the best part of an hour to retrieve the various pieces of the pack, haul them up the slope and restore them to Lady's back. Packing a horse single handed is not easy even under ideal conditions, particularly if the articles are heavy. My task was made the more difficult by the narrowness of the trail. On one side I was high above the horse, and on the other I was well below it. The strain of my exertions began to tell, and things were not improved when I shot between the mare's legs from the high side. And I was taking a dim view of things when I fell on my face for the sixth time while working from the low side of the animal.

When the pack was finally secured it was distinctly out of balance, but I was at least able to resume the journey. Paint, I am sure, was sorry that the affair had ended, for I am convinced that she came as near as a horse can to grinning while I was struggling to restore the position.

Happily, the damage sustained was slight. Of the twelve dozen eggs, a few were cracked, but not one was broken, and Lady was none the worse for her fall. But time had been lost, and I was well behind schedule when I left the pass behind. Down in the valley the snow had vanished except where it had drifted very deeply and where the trees were very tall and dense. Being much higher than Colston, however, the snow reached far down the slopes, only the trail at the bottom of the valley being quite clear.

I was now in my own district, but still twenty miles from my main cabin at Wind Lake. I had meant to reach journey's end in time for a late lunch, but the unlooked for delay caused by Lady induced me to resort to a rarely used cabin at the foot of the pass. There I relieved the horses of their loads and loosened their girths, allowing them to nibble at what grass there was nearby. I had made no provision for camping en route, and my supplies were so well packed that it would have entailed a major operation to reach the items needed to make a meal.

Having blunted the edge of my hunger with a bar of chocolate and a cigarette, I had a drink of clear, icy water from the creek. As I expected, the telephone in the cabin failed to produce a sound. The line, strung on short poles over the pass, had completely disappeared, having been swept to the bottom of the ravine in one of the winter snow slides. This happened every winter, the line being broken in several places. It was useless trying to do anything about it until most of the snow had gone, and as there would be no danger of forest fires for several weeks, the phone was not likely to be needed.

My journey along the valley ran for several miles almost parallel with the one I had left on the other side of the range. Here, however, there were no motor cars, for we were deep in the wild, no human foot having trod the trails since my little cavalcade had left the district in the previous fall. Nor was there likelihood of visitors for some weeks, and perhaps not until the fishing season opened in the middle of June.

For some distance the telephone line to Wind Lake showed no signs of damage. It was strung loosely from tree to tree, threaded through china insulators. Thus, when a tree fell across it, it took up the slack without breaking it. Coming upon a stretch of tight line I knew that there was a windfall not far ahead. It proved to be a big tree that would take some cutting out. Usually such windfalls blocked the trail, being too high to climb over and with their ends lying in a tangle of fallen trees or in thick undergrowth, and occasionally against a precipitous hill side. Luckily we were able to make our way round this one, but I was aware that it was unwise to rely on making the journey in the normal six or seven hours when entering the reserve in spring. It was prudent to journey with everything available to make camp and with food readily available for two or three meals.

It was essential to make as much haste as possible. I was reminded of this as we neared the southern turn in the valley. A dull roar, increasing in sound and becoming ever more ominous as we advanced, warned that the creek would not be easy to cross.

Normally the stream presented no obstacle. In summer, although it was forty feet wide, it was not more than two feet deep even in the centre. But a long warm day had melted immense quantities of snow, and the mounting roar announced that the waters were unusually high. Paint snorted and all three horses pricked up their ears in alarm.

When the creek came into view its rushing waters looked formidable. Now twice as wide as usual, they had submerged the steep banks, and in the centre, where the current was at its strongest, large waves ridged up, giving the surface an angry appearance. Had I reached the creek an hour later I should have made no attempt to cross it, for the waters were rising steadily, and not far below was a jam of windfalls, and to be swept into them might well have cost the life of a horse or even my own life.

Anticipating that the creek would be fairly high, I had taken the precaution of packing on top any goods that might suffer damage from water. The pack covers were tightly lashed down, and as the packs would tend to float up a bit, there was little danger that my belongings would suffer injury, particularly as negotiating the deepest part should take only a short time. Nevertheless, I viewed the boiling waters with some trepidation.

Knowing there was some risk in the venture, but having no wish to make camp for the night when my journey's end was so near, I put Paint to the water. Being a venturesome animal she entered without hesitation, and for several yards, although she was being pressed steadily downstream, she was able to keep her feet. When she lost touch with the bed of the creek, I got a wet shirt, but that was all. For she soon got purchase again, and scrambled out on the other side. Nevertheless, the current had carried us downstream a distance of some fifty yards. Barney was close behind, his pack riding high, but being taller than Paint he had not been carried down the creek any distance.

Lady, however, had not found the courage to enter the water. Either because she had been temporarily unnerved by her mishap in the pass or because she knew the current did not suit her ample figure, she was trotting up and down on the far bank, whinnying and making quite a fuss. She hated being parted from her comrades, and to hurry her up, I made as though to move off without her. That did it. She rushed into the water, but being shorter in the leg than the other two, and boasting a considerable girth, she was soon off her feet swimming. She was carried so far downstream, however, that I became alarmed, as the bank for which she was heading was undercut. I rode towards where she would try to come out, unshipping my lariat as I did so. But I had no need to use it. Her attempts to gain a footing on the overhanging bank caused it to collapse, thus allowing her to gain a hold and scramble out. Paint, as though disappointed that the show was over, bucked skittishly and shook her head. She was that kind of a horse.

Without further hindrance we reached the cabin, and I thrilled to the sight of it. This was to be my home for

ST2*

the next six months, and I loved it. The horses, relieved of their loads and trappings, had a good roll and then made off for the rich pasture at the bottom of the valley. Usually where the ground was clear of trees, there was bog or muskeg, but down there, on either side of the creek, there was good green grass.

A stack of dry logs and plenty of kindling made ready in the previous fall soon provided a cheerful roaring fire in the stove and a much needed meal was under way. When unpacking my stores to stack them away I found they had suffered but little harm. The ends of my sleeping bag were wet and many of the canned goods were losing their labels. So I took the precaution of marking their contents on the tins, having been caught that way once before. It is annoying to open a can expecting to find sausages and to be greeted with the pleasant but disappointing aroma of strawberries.

As there was an ample supply of spare blankets in the cabin, I put the sleeping bag, the saddles and their ropes and girths out to dry.

On strolling down to Wind Lake I came upon Annie, a cow moose who was an essential part of the scenery, if not of attractive appearance. She was in the shallows, her head under water, feeding on aquatic plants. Up came her large unlovely head, lavishly decorated with dripping weed. She eyed me for several seconds, decided that she had seen me before, and returned her ugly, friendly countenance to the water. No doubt she would soon pay the horses a visit, for she was an old friend of theirs.

Out in the lake there still floated a few miniature icebergs, and although vast quantities of water poured into it from the swollen creek it was little above its normal level. I had rather expected to see Annie with an offspring, as she usually produced one in the early spring. Perhaps she had neglected her courting the previous year, or maybe a cougar or a wolf had accounted for it. Whatever the reason, Annie was alone.

Returning to the cabin, I found my equipment dry

enough to hang in its usual place, and feeling ready to
eat again, I made myself another meal. Although it was
not yet dark, I was ready for bed. Like the horses, I was
not yet broken to the trail. But, with the dishes washed,
I could not resist a smoke on the verandah, to revel for a
few minutes in the beauty and the solitude. The wild
provides a rich companionship of its own. There is a
profound sense of presence, which perhaps explains why
the hermit finds his life so attractive.

In addition, there was Barney's bell intermittently
punctuating the silence; Annie making her ungainly way
in that direction, a doe timidly stepping into the cabin
clearing, the cry of a loon and the honk of geese echoing
across the lake as they sought a resting place for the
night. The geese were, indeed, birds of passage, pausing
but briefly on their long journey to the far north.

The piping of a bluebird told me that the usual pair
had arrived for the summer. Every year they raised a
family beneath the eaves of the cabin. Once, I saw them
end their journey from the south. After preening themselves in the sun for a time, the hen bird hopped to the
eaves to the exact site of the nest, showing not the least
hesitation. She peeped into the old nest, and the cock
bird joined her. Together they examined their former
habitation, and evidently decided that it would not do
for a further season. For the next day they were busy
bringing in all the soft materials they could find.

At the end of the warm day the air was heavy with the
scent of pine needles, and the lake, a mirror reflecting all
the magic of the surrounding peaks, broke as a trout rose,
re-forming to picture once again the snow capped summits.
The colours in the rays of the setting sun ranged from a
delicate pink to deep salmon, changing and deepening
as the shadows crept across the valley.

A pair of diminutive fawns hesitantly followed their
mother into the clearing, poised ready for instant flight
should there be the least cause for alarm.

Thus the end of my first day of the season was as
perfect as it could be. It was too early for the mosquitoes

to be at their teasing, and I knew that there would be many more such endings to the day in the near future.

There was a radio in the cabin, but I was not drawn to it. I was glad to be free of the clamour of civilisation. The street cars, movie shows, the strident advertisements, the rack and tension of the scramble for dollars. Above all, I was not forced to listen to someone else's radio, unavoidable in town, any more than I was compelled to listen to my own.

I rose to put out a block of salt. Ostensibly I had brought this for the horses, but the creatures of the wild were more in need of it than they. My move caused the doe and fawns to leap away, but they soon returned, and the doe licked hungrily at the salt, a commodity in short supply in the Rockies, and one which the animals appreciated greatly. By that mysterious means by which news travels in the forests, it was soon widely known that salt was available. And to it, with astonishing speed, came a variety of creatures, each claiming a share and competing with all the rest for a satisfying lick.

All night, and for several nights, there would be noisy squabbling at the salt block, many of the creatures shedding their natural caution in order to secure what they needed. Once their craving was satisfied, however, they would again exercise their customary discretion.

A last look over Wind Lake revealed a mountain sheep and two lambs barely discernible on a high ledge wending their precarious way to still greater heights. I had seen it many times before, but the scene never lost its fascination.

I was awakened by the horses moving about outside the cabin, nickering to inform me that they had come for their ration of oats. This early morning delicacy had not been forgotten, though six months of winter divided them from the last time they had received it. The practice was one which saved me what might have been a very long walk to bring them in on the days that I needed them. But today they could spend leisurely, eating grass, for I had much to do about the house.

The first job of the season was trail clearing and repairing the telephone line. The phone extended no farther than Wind Lake, but the trails threaded their way over a distance of a hundred miles. The main one, leading to Sikanaska, wound from top to bottom of the district and was nearly sixty miles long. There were several side trails for which I was responsible, and they had to be in good shape ready for the tourists who would be coming along later, but clear trails were vital should there be a fire. Over them, at top speed, would come the men and equipment who would have to deal with any serious outbreak. Every delay on the trail allows fire to make headway, giving a blaze the chance to become a conflagration.

Not for some weeks would the forest become dangerously dry, but the respite would be needed, for the winter storms, fierce and sometimes lasting for days, often produced a crop of windfalls. On occasion there were several to the mile, some of considerable size, and each fallen tree had to be cut out and removed from the trail. In this region, there was land enough and time enough, at least until there was the danger of fire. Then there would be days of hard riding and hours of acute anxiety.

Trail clearing and line fixing called for an early start. By the afternoon the creeks had risen to difficult and even dangerous levels. And so it was that I made an early breakfast, and one which the most luxurious hotels could not surpass. For what can be better than bacon, flapjacks, and coffee, their mingled aroma drifting in the living air of the Rockies?

And so, on the second morning, having breakfasted regally, I started out with a light pack on Barney, with Lady tagging along because she refused to be left behind. The day would come when the hot sun would bring anxiety, and I would scour my district with apprehensive eyes, fearful of detecting the wisp of smoke that would announce that a fire had been started in a forest where scores of thousands of trees were oven dry. But those anxious days were in the future. At the moment my attention was claimed by the journey from Wind Lake to the far south of the district, a distance of fully forty miles. Black Lake marked the halfway line of the journey, and there was an unpretentious cabin. It lacked the amenities of my headquarters, but there was a clearing with feed for the horses and it made it unnecessary to erect a tent. At the Sikanaska Lakes near the southern end of my region was another cabin almost as well arranged and equipped as the one at Wind Lake.

The first few miles of the trail followed the contours of the lake. A few minor windfalls called for the use of the axe, but they were disposed of without difficulty. When we crossed the creek at the end of the lake it was quite low. During the night there had been frost high up, and it was still too early for the snow to have started melting. On the other side of the creek was a large open space, level and fairly free of timber, which I called the cross-roads. The name was suggested by the four valleys which fanned out from the clearing, a large peak standing sentinel at each corner. There was the valley from which we had come, a second continuing south, a third extending to the west, while the fourth, which led to Black Lake, took a south easterly direction. From the south and turning to the west was the Cougar River.

The Cougar River was of some size and it eventually turned back to the east, dropping down to the Cougar Valley in which lay the town of Colston. But the water found a way which was barred to man, unless he had the agility and certainty of foot usually reserved to the mountain goat. On entering the valley to the west the river passed between sheer cliffs, the gorge being narrower than the average width of the river. Here the waters piled up angrily, impatient to be on their way. The gorge that morning was a smother of boiling, surging water, but it would be much higher later in the day. Fed by some fifty creeks, all of which would swell under the growing impact of the melting snows, the river would rise in depth and savagery.

I decided that the other side could wait for my attention. The horses might have crossed safely, but they were

bound to be swept far downstream before they gained
the other side. And if they failed to make the river's width
before being thrust to the gorge, nothing could save them.
Once, having wintered in this district, I saw the gorge in
early spring. The ice had just broken up and was piled
there in huge masses, presenting a thrilling, fear-inspiring
sight.

Entering Black Lake valley I came upon a heavy stand
of spruce. Here, in winter, snow piled to a depth of more
than twenty feet. The long standing growth of timber was
tall and thick, the trees rising in long graceful columns on
every side and imposing a cathedral-like stillness. But the
chipmunk and the spruce partridge were not impressed
by it. The chipmunk broke the quiet with its busy chip
chip, while the partridge was so impervious to its surroundings that it was indulging in a courting dance in the
bole of a tree which had been down for several years. The
acoustics were so perfect that his pounding wings echoed
through the forest like a signal drum in the depths of the
Congo.

Snow still lingered in this cool, shaded place. It had
been so deep in the winter that even the frost of down to
sixty degrees below zero had been unable to penetrate
to the forest floor. Proof of this was provided by the
splashes of mauve and purple where clustered crocuses
had pushed their heads above the snow. Shafts of sunlight thrust through the foliage, accentuating the colour
against the pure white background.

Ahead across the trail was an immense windfall forming an impassable barrier. Fully two feet thick and some
three feet above the ground, each end was lost in a tangle
of smaller windfalls. There was nothing for it but to go
to work on it with axe and saw. This was no mean task,
and maybe some might have tackled it with axe alone.
Judging that to be beyond my powers I dismounted, and
the horses, as though realising that they would be
stationary for some time, stood at ease and promptly
dozed.

Withdrawing my axe from its scabbard and taking the

" Swede " saw from beneath the pack cover, I assembled it and surveyed my task. The saw would cut through no more than a third of the trunk before the tubular bow fouled the tree. Then, as the weight was resting on branches, the cut would close like a vice, imprisoning the saw. The job called for a long, stout pole and some sort of fulcrum.

Within ten minutes the saw had cut as deeply as it would go. Cutting a deep V with the axe, I resumed sawing but, halfway through, the saw bound so tightly that it was immovable. Finding a strong pole some twenty-five feet in length, I then cut off a forked branch into which I could fit the pole. With the branch about two and a half feet high, I inserted the pole end firmly under the tree and with my fulcrum close up it required little effort to lift the two tons of tree so that the cut opened to half an inch. To anchor the pole while I continued sawing presented a further problem. Providentially a large root crossed the trail, and I burrowed a hole beneath it, thrust into it the end of the pole and secured it to the root with my lariat. By enlarging the V in the cut, I was soon wielding a freely running saw. On cutting through, the butt end remained above the ground, still across the trail. This helped, as there was no need to hold it up while I cut from it the six feet or so needed to clear the trail.

With the cut kept open by its own weight, cutting off the necessary length took but little time. With a piece cut from my pole serving as a lever, I had the length of tree I had cut out off the trail within a few minutes. But the windfall had set me back some two hours, and I hoped there would be no more like it before I reached Black Lake.

Rousing the horses, I continued, this time carrying the saw in case it was needed. We encountered nothing but small obstacles, however, and it was barely past noon when we arrived at Black Lake. But I meant to go no farther that day. There was not much grass in the clearing by the cabin beyond a fair amount of last year's growth which had cured on the stalk into indifferent hay. With this and their ration of oats, however, the horses would make do, and having seen to their needs, I made myself an urgently needed meal.

I was eating and gazing out of the window when I saw a black fox trotting up the trail. A beautiful animal, and exceedingly rare, it is greatly coveted by the trapper. My visitor halted some distance from the cabin, one foot poised as he carefully examined the horses. Turning his attention to the cabin and deciding that it was no longer unoccupied, he turned tail and vanished in a trice.

My next visitor was a porcupine which I had encountered on previous visits to Black Lake. Unlike the cautious fox, he ambled through the open door, apparently quite oblivious of my presence, grumbling away to himself in typical porcupine fashion. I tossed him a piece of bread, which he examined, approved and devoured. Then, having made a tour of the cabin, he departed, still grumbling as if his life gave him cause for unending complaint.

I also caught sight of several deer and an elk. These, however, were as wary as the fox. Sensing that the cabin was tenanted, they left the trail, making their way past it by a detour that gave it a very wide berth. No bears came to sniff inquisitively about the place. But they would be around later. At the moment, their winter fast over, they would be replenishing empty stomachs on the young grass, shoots and buds growing on the southern slopes.

Black Lake was well named, for it had the appearance of ink. Nevertheless, it was crystal clear when looked into from close by. It was of great depth and half enclosed by sheer grey rock which accounted for its dark sheen. There was quite a lot of thick ice floating about, the white sharply contrasting with the black background. The lake, which was right on the divide, had a creek flowing from each end. One found its way to the Cougar River, the other to the Sikanaska. It was fed by a torrent gushing out from the rock on the far side. This must have

been fed by a glacier hidden away in the massive range
to the south, as it kept flowing freely throughout the
summer.

A number of duck were in evidence, determined, it
seemed, to rest there for the night, and trout were on the
move, leaping from the dark depths. Black Lake was
beautiful, but there was a hint of the sinister in its loveli-
ness.

I made an early start the next day. I had a few windfalls to clear, but nothing that caused me any trouble.
Thus I had leisure to notice a remarkable change in the
scenery, and a change which had taken place since the
previous summer. The transformation had occurred about
half way to Sikanaska. Some twenty years before, fire had
ravaged about a mile of the south side of the valley.
Along the steep slope rose a forest of poles, naked and
bereft of their bark, grey, dead, and depressing.

That was the scene the previous year. But the empty
poles stood no longer. Their roots having become too
decayed to support them any longer, a winter snow slide
had started moving them from the top, and building up
tremendous pressure, had swept the whole lot down into
the valley. The enormous momentum had forced them
well out on to the flat for a long distance in a heap fifty
feet high. For some three hundred yards it completely
hid the creek, a huge pile of thousands of tons of
timber. It was, of course, impossible to move it from such
an inaccessible spot, and there it would remain an additional fire hazard during the summer heat.

I crossed the creek and, later, the Sikanaska, with dry
feet. A ride of some six or seven miles along the lower
lake brought me to the cabin at the southern end. There
were few windfalls, and the lake with its magnificent
background of lofty peaks was a sight which commanded
the attention without any risk of it ever wearying.

A hen spruce partridge fluttered out from the side of
the trail, and, as if injured, flopped along a few feet in
advance of my horse. The performance, however, was not

new to me, and looking to the point where she had first
appeared, I saw her nest, as I had expected. From it quite
a crowd of chicks were taking off in all directions. Some,
which tried to alight on twigs, were unable to maintain
their balance and hung upside down. Some had been
hatched so recently that they were scarcely dry, and none
had had flying experience. Yet they could fly after a
fashion, and awareness of danger had been hatched along
with them.

The hen bird continued acting as though injured until
I was some fifty yards from the nest. Then, satisfied that
her performance had drawn me far enough away from
her brood, she " recovered " and flew swiftly back to her
nest.

This trick of drawing an intruder away from the nest
by acting as if injured is not peculiar to the spruce partridge. It was performed for me later that same day.
Having reached the cabin and satisfied myself that all
was in order, I went to the lakeside. This time the bird
was a dipper, which flew almost from beneath my feet,
behaving as if injured. The dipper is a snipe-like water
bird which sits on a rock bobbing up and down like a
jack-in-the-box, then diving and remaining submerged
so long you begin to think it will never come up again.
Had I watched the antics of the bird I should certainly
have missed the brood from which she had intended to
distract my attention. Their bodies were no larger than
my finger nail, but their legs and beaks were so long and
delicate that it was a wonder they did not snap. Their
colouring was so exactly like the stones among which
they had scattered that if they stopped moving or I took
my eyes off them for a second, it was impossible to discover them again.

I noticed numbers of large trout only partially submerged moving at speed across the shallow bar of a creek
at the point where it entered the lake. They were en route
for their spawning grounds in the highest reaches of the
creek.

Having examined the four trails leading from Sikanaska

to the limits for which I was responsible, I returned to
Wind Lake, completing the journey in a single day. I still
had another forty miles or so of trail to fix and the telephone line to repair as soon as the Pass and Cougar River
allowed me access to them. The boat on Wind Lake,
powered by an outboard motor, would also need overhauling, the cabin needed a little attention, there were
logs to haul in and wood to cut, and there were such
chores as baking bread and mending torn clothing.

I was nearing the cabin on my return to Wind Lake
when the horses halted suddenly and snorted nervously.
They had good reason to, for there was a bear not far
from the cabin rummaging about between a couple of
large windfalls which served as a garbage dump. One of
the largest grizzlies, he was an old acquaintance whose
size had surprised several who had much more experience
of bears than I had. He had his winter hideout somewhere
north of the lake and passed through Wind Lake every
spring on the way to his summer stamping ground,
returning over the same route each fall. He often lingered
in the neighbourhood for a day or two, and, at first, he
had given me some anxious moments. But I had grown
used to him, although the horses were alarmed by any
bear we encountered. The bear raised his enormous head,
regarded us curiously for a moment, and then quietly
ambled out of sight.

II : BEAR TROUBLE

My years in the Rockies gave me ample opportunity to study the creatures of the wild, and my understanding of them bred in me a reluctance to kill any animal or bird unless it was absolutely necessary. The rifle I carried was a high power .22; it was not the type of weapon with which to tackle a grizzly bear or a moose, and it was only rarely that there was occasion to shoot these animals.

The rifle, however, was powerful enough to account for coyotes, wolves and cougars. These were the animals whose numbers had to be kept to the minimum, otherwise they made serious inroads on lesser creatures. The Indians, fortunately for me, were experts in dealing with the predatory animals, and in all my years as a Ranger I shot only one cougar, a couple of wolves and a few coyotes. On occasion other animals demanded my attention, either because they interfered with me directly or because they threatened the lives of visitors to the reserve.

Bears, though normally more inquisitive than hostile, caused me no little trouble that summer. In fact, I was called upon to deal with them on no less than three occasions.

The first occurred when I returned from a trip which

had kept me away from my Wind Lake headquarters for a couple of days. I was made aware that something was wrong as I rode to the porch of the cabin. The horses made it plain that they had no wish to approach the hitch rail, although they had never displayed any reluctance before. I could see nothing amiss, and a look round revealed nothing to cause the uneasiness, but it was with no little effort that I eventually persuaded the horses to the rail. I unsaddled and removed the pack, but they still would not settle, continuing to snort and fidget. I concluded that a bear had recently been roaming about the cabin, his scent still being strong enough to disturb the horses.

Having turned them loose, I entered the cabin to stand in shocked amazement as I pushed open the door. There had been a bear all right, and he had not been content to stay outside the cabin. The window on the far side along with its frame had been ripped out, and the interior of my headquarters was a shambles. The store cupboard had been torn open and its contents tumbled all over the floor. Cans of milk, fruit and syrup had been neatly punctured by sharp teeth and the contents sucked out. The table was overturned, and on the floor lay blankets, radio, stove pipe and every movable object.

In the midst of an inextricable mixture of soot, flour, lard and other items, the intruder had tarried to chew on a large lump of bacon. This had given him some trouble, and while struggling with it, the mixture amidst which he had been standing had been well stirred and quantities of bacon fat had been added to it.

I was aghast. Much of my food reserve had been ruined and the mess was indescribable. Not having eaten for several hours, I was exceedingly hungry. I set up the bent stove pipe, salvaged a few items and prepared some sort of a meal and boiled up some coffee. It was difficult to know where to make a start on the clearing up. At least a full day was needed, plus extra time in which to wash the blankets. I was eating my meal and pondering where to make a start on the cabin when there was a scuffle

behind me. And there was a very young bear trying to
scramble in through the window. Despite the fact that
he was a mere infant, his bulk filled the window space,
and when he hesitated on seeing me, I persuaded him to
retire by throwing a wash basin at him.

It was obvious, however, that the bear had to be
destroyed. Now that he had tasted such delicacies as
syrup, milk and bacon, and enjoyed himself wrecking the
place, he would come again and again. Growing quickly,
he would also achieve a size and strength of such proportions that he would find it child's play to take the cabin
apart.

I was satisfying myself that my .22 rifle had the power
to account for a bear of such a size, when he tried to enter
the cabin again, this time by way of the door. I threw a
log at him and hit him on the nose, and he responded by
belligerently baring his teeth before retiring. It was
obvious that he not only had to be destroyed, but that he
must be disposed of without delay. A brown bear of some
two hundred pounds, a shot in the right place would fix
him. Taking up my rifle, I went to the door, to find that
he was already advancing on the cabin once again. I had
never before known a bear act in this way. Even full
grown visitors who had every reason to be aggressive
usually took a hint and retired, and more often they kept
at a respectful distance.

He was some twenty yards from me, his head down in
a stiff-necked sort of attitude, snorting angrily, when I
fired. The bullet struck him in the forehead just above the
eyes. He went down like a log, never to move again. As
he was in the moulting stage, his skin was of no value,
and not being keen on bear meat, I dragged the body
away, knowing that the scavengers of the wild would
quickly deal with it.

I spent the whole of the following day straightening
up, and I got my blankets washed, but three-quarters of
my food stocks had been ruined or had vanished. Having
rescued the items that were still intact, I rang up Pete
McLean and told him what had happened. It was impos-
ST3

sible for me to spare a couple of days making the trip into town, but I was lucky. A party of anglers were coming out next day, and Pete said he would let them have an extra horse to bring up the supplies I needed. I had quite a long list of requirements, but they arrived all right the next day.

I not only repaired the ruined window, but spiked some stout poles across it, and then protected the other windows in the same way.

There was more trouble with a bear when a party of tourists consisting of a man, wife and two teen age children arrived at my cabin in a very disturbed state of mind. They had not had a guide with them, and they had encountered plenty of trouble with slipping packs and straying horses. Then, to ruin their vacation, they had encountered bear trouble, and the man was lucky to be alive.

Age makes some people obstinate and difficult, and it seems to affect animals the same way. This is particularly the case, it appears, with animals which have led protected lives. They lose what little fear of humans they have ever had and come to resent their presence.

Evidently this is what had happened to the bear which had frightened this family of tourists very badly. She was well known down Sikanaska way as being fairly tame. She would remain within sight of travellers, only showing temper when chased by dogs. This time, however, she had run amok.

The day before, the family had returned to their tent to find it torn to shreds and a large black bear in possession, playing havoc with their belongings. Normally bears are quite harmless unless they are wounded or provoked. This bear, however, contrary to her normal habit, took umbrage when an effort was made to drive her away.

Seeing their belongings were being wrecked, and having been told that bears were not belligerent, the man rushed at the animal brandishing a piece of wood. He struck the bear on the head, but instead of making off, she let out a roar and charged. The man fled, the bear in hot

BEAR TROUBLE 35

pursuit. Lashing out, she ripped his belt and tore his trousers. Fortunately, he managed to reach a tree and shoot up it. Later, when I saw this tree, I marvelled that this man, who was the rather portly city type, had managed to make his way up it. He looked as if he would have experienced difficulty climbing a ladder. Yet he had shinned up a dead tree which was without bark, covering fifteen feet of smooth trunk before reaching a branch. How he had managed I do not know; neither did the man himself.

Even the bear had not been able to follow him, but had remained at the base of the tree, clawing at the trunk and making threatening noises. The position of the traveller was anything but enviable, for he had climbed to the highest branches, where, minus his pants, he had to stay for several hours. Throughout a period that seemed to him to last an eternity, his family, at a discreet distance, added to his misery by shouting useless and even ridiculous advice. Even after the bear had departed to pursue more lawful business, the hapless visitor had remained a long time in the tree. When he finally returned to terra firma, he and his family had the nerve-racking task of hunting their scattered horses, which had fled when the bear approached. Then, packing with all haste, they had travelled all night, arriving in a state of great weariness and tension.

Having told them that they could rest and eat at the cabin, I phoned Pete McLean, who agreed that the bear would have to be destroyed. As it was a big bear and my .22 rifle was not equal to it, he promised to send me a .303 and some shells with the next person who happened to be passing through Wind Lake. Meanwhile, I was to warn travellers to avoid the danger area.

The rifle arrived a few days later, but only three shells came with it plus the message that they were all Pete had and there were no more to be had in Colston.

When I arrived in the region where the bear had shown fight I found a party of tourists camped there. They wished to stay at the lake near where the bear had its

ST3*

domain, but having been warned of the danger, they had awaited my arrival. Now they followed me en masse to see the fun.

I set out in search of the bear, the audience at my heels. This rather embarrassed me, serving to distract my attention, causing me to imagine I had caught sight of her when there was no sign of her. I looked to my rifle, told the onlookers to stay where they were, and casually remarked that I'd feel more content had my ammunition not been limited to only three shells.

Looking round a few moments later I found that I was quite alone. The tourists had retreated to their camp, and were content to remain there until the matter was concluded.

I saw nothing of the bear that day, but the following midday I caught sight of her. She did not retire, and she favoured me with a look that showed that she was in anything but a friendly humour. I wanted to be near enough to make reasonably sure that the first shell would be sufficient, but not too near if my marksmanship proved faulty. I was within fifty yards of her, manœuvring to get her side on to me, but she turned steadily, thus constantly facing me. Although she was snuffling fiercely and regarding me with a marked hostility, she did not

advance, but I felt sure that at any moment she would make a move with the intention of seeing me off.

Something must have momentarily caught her attention, for she turned and presented her side to me. I fired and down she went, but for no more than a second. Scrambling to her feet with a roar of rage, she came at me. With only two shells in my magazine and with a wounded bear as heavy as a horse lumbering towards me I should certainly have been scared had I had the time to realise my position. But acting instinctively, I fired again, and although I no longer had a steady target, the shell struck her between the neck and shoulder. She went down for a second time, and made no effort to rise again. Nevertheless, it was some time before I approached her, and even then with my finger on the trigger, ready to discharge my last shell. There was, however, no further need for caution, as she was dead, and it seemed that the first shell was the one which had done the most damage. It had entered just behind the shoulder and must have passed very near to the heart. The pelt proved to be of no worth, being very worn and mangy.

The campers were the richer by the claws which they removed as souvenirs.

A third bear gave trouble later in the season, but a moose demanded attention before I was called on to come to terms with the bear. The moose was no stranger to me, and he was a fine specimen, but age was making him crotchety and cantankerous. For two or three years he had shown himself unwilling to allow visitors right of way when they met him on the trail. His obstinacy was still more pronounced during the rutting season, at which time I had come upon him once or twice. On each occasion I had avoided coming to issue with him, but tourists were likely to fall foul of him, and it became obvious that sooner or later he was bound to cause trouble.

It was more than probable that a younger bull had designs on his stamping ground, and if that was the case he was certain to become exceedingly savage, particularly if he was compelled to give up his privileges.

It was in the fall that an incident occurred which made it evident that he could be allowed to live no longer. He attacked a string of horses belonging to a fairly large party of tourists. A dozen or so pack horses were tied nose to tail, and they were on their way to Black Lake when the old moose went berserk. The riders who were free were able to avoid him, but the pack horses could do nothing to get out of his way. Frightened, they tangled with one another, and half of them were knocked off their feet. Luckily, all of them escaped with nothing worse than cuts and scratches, the guide and horse wrangler managed to drive off the moose by striking him with poles.

" It was a right mess," said the wrangler, who came to report the matter. " Unless something is done about that critter someone is going to get killed."

Bound to agree, I took the .303, for which I now had more shells, and set out in search of the moose. I detested having to kill him, for he was a fine creature, an old friend, and he added to my reluctance by waiting docilely until I approached within a hundred yards. Fortunately one shot was enough, and he died on the instant. As a memorial to a fine creature of the wilds, his skull and splendid spread of antlers decorate the porch of Wind Lake cabin.

My surmise concerning a younger bull proved correct, for he appeared frequently in the same area the following season.

I was on my way back to the ranch in the fall when I encountered the third bear. It was my custom to spend the night with a Ranger whose district I passed through, and on this occasion he told me that one of his horses had died. That morning he had gone out with the intention of disposing of the carcase, only to find that it had vanished.

" Come out here," he said, " and see what happened."

From where the dead horse had been there was a wide trail revealing that it had been dragged away. This led down a steep ravine and up the other side, where bushes and undergrowth had been flattened by its passage. The horse, in fact, had been transported a good quarter of a mile before being partially eaten.

This could only be the work of a bear, but it could only be a bear of exceptional size and strength. The horse weighed in the region of eight hundred pounds and would have taxed the strength of another horse to drag its dead weight on the level. Yet the bear had man-handled it up a bush covered ravine which had a slope of forty-five degrees.

The grizzly having once sampled horseflesh was likely to want more, and my friend was by no means anxious to have a bear rambling around which might attack his horses. He asked if I would help him hunt the animal down, and, armed with rifles of the necessary calibre, we set out the next morning.

It was cold and the ground was thickly carpeted with frost. The trees, too, were filmed with white, and while the scene was compellingly beautiful, it provided a back-ground against which a grizzly bear is almost invisible. We approached the remains of the horse cautiously. The bear had made a second feed on it during the night, and the very fresh tracks in the rime indicated that he had left only as we approached.

The Ranger suggested that we should move in the direction of the tracks; he followed them, while I kept some fifty yards away. We moved forward carefully, and while keeping my distance I was able to catch a glimpse of the Ranger from time to time. To tell the truth, I was feeling rather nervous, for the bear would be hard to distinguish at any distance, and I had no wish suddenly to discover him at very close quarters.

We reached a place that was fairly clear of brush. There my companion stopped and was motioning me to do the same. I stared hard ahead, but could see no sign of the bear. Then a slight movement drew my eye and there he was. Erect and looking in our direction, he was some eighty yards away, his silver tipped coat blending per-fectly with the frosted bush. My friend drew a careful bead and the air exploded deafeningly as he fired. The grizzly slumped in a heap, then rose on his forelegs, his back legs evidently paralysed. He looked exceedingly unpleasant, his fierce eyes searching for his enemy.

I heard the Ranger work another shell into his rifle. The bear heard him, too, and with a roar he sped towards the sound. Although his hind legs were useless, he made plenty of ground. Tearing over the clearing at a speed which amazed and terrified, he did not so much as check when the Ranger loosed another shell at him. I opened up, but the need for haste reduced the effectiveness of my aim. Nevertheless, two of the bullets struck the bear. Now, however, he was only seven or eight yards from the Ranger, who fired yet a third shell into him. The bear halted then, lurched and fell almost at the feet of my friend. The Ranger had been on the point of running, but he would have been much too late, for I should not have dared to fire for fear of bringing him down and not the bear. In any case, he would have been overtaken in a matter of seconds and savaged to death just as quickly.

The skin, which measured nine feet, was in perfect condition. I saw it often after that covering a large part of the living-room at the Ranger station. We were never able to decide whose shot finally put paid to the bear, but he was certainly tough, for three of the shells had struck him in spots which should have proved fatal. The grizzly takes a great deal of killing.

III : DUTCH WAS NEUTRAL

DUTCH GREEN was one of a number of guides who frequented my area. Although we met only rarely, we became quite friendly, and on one occasion he took the opportunity to tell me something of his life in the Rockies, a life which perhaps no one else has ever quite equalled.

There had been a long dry spell and I was out on patrol, on the alert for fires, my mount the fast walking Barney. It was my intention to make Sikanaska, then return the same day, and while it was no mean distance, it was necessary to cover as much ground as possible during a dry spell, when the risk of an outbreak of fire was at its greatest.

I had become so used to the sun's daily march across the heavens, that I had left my slicker, which was generally tied to my saddle, behind. When I first heard the thunder in the mountains and saw the black clouds building up, I paid them little heed. This had happened several times in the past few weeks and nothing had come of it. This time, however, the heavens opened, giving me a thorough soaking.

Confident that the storm must have saturated the whole area, thus eliminating all danger of fire, I turned back. The clouds arched the sky as far as I could see, and the

rain continued until I reached the shelter of my cabin.
But someone else had found shelter there before me, as
the string of pack horses outside testified.

My visitor was Dutch Green, who appeared to be
almost as wet as I was.

" Going some place?" I greeted him.

" Not in this lot," he said. " I have a bunch of mountain
climbers parked in British Columbia, just over O'Connor
Pass. I took 'em in the other way and thought I'd come
around this way to get 'em. It makes only a few miles
difference, and I kind of like the scenery hereabouts. I
figured on making Black Lake today, but if it fines up
tomorrow I can make up time."

I threw the saddle off Barney, who set off to find his
pals on the flat. By the time Dutch had sorted out his
string of horses and packed his gear on the porch, I was
changed, had a fire going and a meal ready. From my
wardrobe I took a few items for Dutch to wear while his
own clothes were drying.

It rained all day, and something was said which caused
me to relate some of my experiences in the First World
War.

Dutch grinned.

" I was kinda neutral in those days," he said.

" Neutral!" I exclaimed.

" That surprises you, eh? Let me tell you about it."

It wasn't often Dutch talked about himself, but he
made up for lost time with the yarn he told that day.

" It was back in that war of yours when I got into
trouble," he said. " Not for hoss stealin' or anything like
that, mind you. They wanted to draft me into the Army
and I flatly refused to be drafted. I was wrong, I reckon,
but I was young in those days, a bit wild and highly
independent. My father's name was Gruen, and that was
the way he always spelt it, but we younger ones changed
it to Green. That's how I got the name of Dutch. Dad was
a good man, but a real ironbender. He was as strict as a
monk, and he thought of little else but work. As far as
he was concerned, the Vaterland could do no wrong, but

my three brothers and me figured that we were Canadians and nothing else.

"Anyway, the two eldest weren't drafted as they were working full time on the farm. My other brother was drafted, but because of the German in him they kept him on non-combatant duties. As for me, two years before the war, being unable to see eye to eye with the old man on some important topics, I pulled out and got a job horse wrangling up here in the mountains.

"That's what I was doing when I got my draft notice. I told 'em I was plumb neutral, and that they could do what they liked about it. I was part German and part Canadian, and I'd no intention of joining their golderned Army. Though I was born in this country I still felt the Germans were somehow my own people. It would have been different if they'd been attacking Canada. As it was, I was stubborn, as ornery as hell and determined to stay plumb neutral. I threw the papers out, and when the Police came tried to throw them out as well. But I guess they'd heard about my attitude, and their numbers proved too many for me.

"I was rewarded with six months in the hoosegow. That doesn't sound a long time, but if I didn't change my

mind I knew there'd be another six months and maybe
twelve. Besides, I was used to the open air and the woods
since the time I could walk. I remember going camping in
the bush on my own when I was knee high to a yearling
calf. Then there was the time I'd spent in these mountains. To cabin me behind bricks and iron bars was like
caging an eagle or a cougar. I got a sharp attack of claus-
trophoby the moment that cell door clanged shut on me,
and I knew I'd never stand it and remain in my right
mind.

"When I pulled myself up to the little barred hole they
called a window I could see the mountains, and I near
broke my back trying to tear those bars apart. I spent a
week in there, and it seemed like a year, what with being
alone and having nothing to do. I guess they weren't
properly organised to deal with the draft dodgers. There
was several of us, pacifists, religious fanatics, some just
plain 'yellow' and maybe one or two odd characters like
me. We were allowed to wear our own clothes, and I
suppose we were treated better than ordinary criminals.
But if they'd treated me like royalty I would have
yearned only to be free. Each day I'd look at those mountains and swear no one would ever catch me if only I
could get to them. Even if I starved to death in the open,
I'd rather that than be cooped in the jail. I think I kept
myself sane by figuring how I could get out and what
I'd do if ever I made it.

"I found out that the prison tooth doctor came only
once a week, and he'd plenty to do when he came. So
when any of us misfits needed dental attention we were
taken down town by a prison officer to a dentist there.
Thinking I'd maybe have my chance to get away once I
got outside, I complained that I was suffering from tooth-
ache. Sure enough a guard in plain clothes brought along
my mackinaw jacket and hat and invited me to come
along with him. It was an invitation I didn't need twice.

"'We won't put any bracelets on you,' this chap said
to me. 'And if you walk along with me no one will know
any difference. You won't be embarrassed, see? But don't

try to get away. Maybe you could run faster than me, but you wouldn't get far, and it would only be the worse for you. Understand?'

"I understood all right, but not the way he meant. It was good to be in the open again, but my guard didn't move far from me, and he was ready to make a grab if I tried to make a break for it. It never occurred to me to use violence, for the officer seemed a sound sort of character, and he was only doing his duty. Noticing me looking round over-eagerly, he gripped my arm.

"'Now don't get any ideas, young feller,' he warned.

"We arrived at the dentist's where we had to wait in a room next to the surgery. Soon someone came out of the surgery and a voice called, 'Next, please.'

"'That's you,' said my guard, picking up a magazine and leaving me to go in alone.

"The dentist examined my teeth and smiled.

"'You've one here that could do with filling,' he said. 'But I can see nothing that would cause you discomfort. Still, I guess it's nice to be out for a while.'

"He went to work on the tooth, and he'd finished the drilling and filling when he was called into the next room to answer the phone. I was alone. This was the heaven-sent opportunity for which I'd been praying, and I didn't delay. It was warm and the window was open, and I soon saw that it gave on to a side street with only a short stretch of lawn between. There was no one in sight and, snatching up my coat, I slipped through the window and was in the street, walking the way I wouldn't have to pass the waiting-room window and trying to hurry without appearing to do so.

"I was free, and my mind began to work overtime. At the most I could not expect more than five minutes before my absence was noticed and the alarm given. But they would not know which way I had taken and some time would be lost before they got a proper search organised.

"Heading west down the street, I quickened my pace. It was a small town and within ten minutes its last buildings lay behind me. Leaving the road, I set off across country still heading due west to the mountains beckoning in the distance. Soon I came to a dirt road leading north and south, beyond which was rough ranching country covered with willow brush. This was just the country for me, for so far I had been too much in the open.

"I was on the point of crossing the road when I heard a car approaching. Taking no chances, I dropped into the ditch, near to which was a culvert. As it was dry I slipped under it, being completely out of sight from the road. I heard another car approaching from the opposite direction and, to my horror, it stopped almost on top of the culvert. I heard a door open, and my heart went out of action for a few moments. Although I could not be seen from above, there was just a chance that this was the Reeve of the district inspecting culverts. But my heart set itself going again when a voice said: 'I'll stop this feller and see if he's seen anything. Looks like old man Hogarth in his jalopy.'

"The car I had first heard stopped, and I heard Mr Hogarth say, 'Mornin', Corporal.'

"'I'm looking for a young chap about six foot tall,' the Corporal said. 'Fair hair, Stetson, blue-grey check mackinaw, black shirt, Levis (jeans or overalls), and low-heeled ridin' boots. Seen him?'

"'Ain't seen a soul since I left the ranch,' Hogarth replied.

"'A feller's slipped out of the hoosegow,' said the Corporal. 'They think he might head for the mountains. As you haven't seen him I'll try a bit farther north. He can't have got much farther than this if he came this way.'

"There was a slamming of doors and both cars moved on. So the hunt was on, with the local Mounty much hotter on the trail than he realised.

"It was still early summer, warm and dry, and it would be no hardship for me to take to the bush. I felt good; I was free of those tarnashun iron bars, and I was heading for the sort of country I knew. Pitting my wits against

woodsmen and the rest somehow appealed to me, and
gave zest to the adventure.

" But breakfast lay a long way behind me, and I had
nothing whatever in my pockets, not so much as a cent,
a knife or even a piece of string. Somehow these
deficiencies, and many more, had to be remedied. Luck
had been with me so far, and I had high hopes that something would turn up. Crossing the road, I entered typical
ranching country, which provided me with ample cover.
Through the willow bush I headed north for a couple of
hours, hoping to fox my pursuers who were most probably thinking that I would continue due west.

" Coming to a road that was little more than a good
wagon trail and which led west, I figured that it would
serve a number of ranches and maybe a tiny community
centre in the shape of a store before it petered out on its
way to the mountains. As my pursuers could not be in
every place at once, I decided I'd a reasonable chance of
reaching a ranch house not on the phone where I'd be
sure of a meal. But a phone line on poles roughly following the road indicated there'd be a party line to all the
ranches in the region.

" So far, though, I'd seen only three buildings in the
distance since leaving the town, which was natural in
ranching country. I'd come maybe twenty-five miles, and
was feeling tired and plenty hungry, and still there wasn't
a sign of a building. I didn't fancy a cold, hungry night
with not even a match to light a fire, but it looked as if
things were shaping that way.

" I remember few occasions when I felt as weary as I
did that summer's evening. I turned west alongside the
road, and though it was hard to keep going when off the
track, I was in no danger of running into some feller on a
horse which would make no sound in the soft dust. There
were plenty of corners, too, as if the road had been made
by a man who was tipsy.

" Another mile or so and I came on what I'd half
expected to find. This was a village, consisting of a store-
post office, community hall, church and one extra house.

It showed no signs of life, but the phone led into the store, and I guessed the folk would know of my escape. So I stayed in the bush, watching and waiting.

" A car came the way I'd come. Its driver filled up with gas and came out of the store with some bread, which made me feel hungrier than ever. The storekeeper was about, anyhow, and it was obvious I should have to wait until he was abed before exploring the outhouses in search of some of the many things I needed.

" Then the storekeeper came out of the back door and went to a barn. Opening the doors wide, he drove out a truck and parked it at the front, then he disappeared inside. A minute later the occupant from the only other house came out with a dog, and leaned on his fence. That dog had me worried, but it didn't detect my presence.

" Then the storekeeper and his wife came out, the husband locking the door and pocketing the key.

" ' Anything I can bring you from town, Jim?' he shouted to the man across the way.

" ' I don't think so,' Jim replied.

" ' We shall be a bit late as we may take in a movie,' said the storekeeper. ' But the back door's open should you need anything.'

" Jim acknowledged the information with a wave of his hand, and the truck drove off down the track.

" Providence could not have been kinder. Right to hand was an unguarded country store, which would stock almost everything, and it wasn't even locked against me. I'd never stolen in my life, and I'd no intention of doing so then; but I could help myself, keep account of what I borrowed and pay when I had the chance.

" It was soon quite dark and Jim had retired to his house and soon to his bed. He had taken his dog with him and there was no sign of there being anyone at the store. I approached the place cautiously, but there was not a sound, and the back door yielded as I lifted the latch. A glow showed the stove was still alight, and it was not long before I found some matches on a shelf. Striking one, I discovered an oil lamp on the table, and I lit it, turning it low. I had a look round the store, then examined the other door to find it was fitted with a Yale lock which could be opened from within.

"With my retreat assured should Jim decide to pay the store a visit, I returned to the living-room, found meat, bread, butter and even some coffee still hot on the stove, and settled to a good meal. My hunger satisfied, and never for a moment neglecting to listen for visitors, I went to the store and found an electric torch. This was just the thing to prevent light reaching the window and betraying my presence. I could see Jim's house dimly outlined in the darkness, and would probably see him before he was across the road if he came.

"With a pencil and a pad of paper I began to make a list of all the things as I set them aside, not forgetting to enter a dollar for the meal I had eaten. While in jail I'd mentally listed the things I should need if I ever escaped, and now I was packing flour, bacon, sugar, coffee, beans and baking powder, and many other items of food, although I left out canned goods as they were too heavy to carry. I added thread, needles, fishing line, hooks, a heavy hunting knife, lariat rope, Swede saw, a light axe, billy can and frying pan, enamel mug, tobacco and thousands of cigarette papers.

"I packed all these things in a sack in the living-room after each trip to the store, topping it up with a change of underclothes, some mocassins and a dozen pairs of socks. I made a rough pack by tying the corners of the sack top to bottom with cord, that way making shoulder loops. It was then that I spotted a .30 rifle, and there were shells for it in the store. I was sorry at taking it, for maybe the feller prized it, but I was only borrowing it, and the hundred shells I took to go with it would be paid for along with the rest of the stuff.

"With such a haul I was almost assured of success in my determination to avoid recapture. My pack was heavy and none too comfortable, though a couple of Hudson Bay blankets acted as a back pad and levelled off the bumps. I covered the lot with a slicker in case of rain and, carrying the rifle and the axe in one hand, a carton of matches in the other, I set out. I was scared they might be crushed and catch light in the pack, destroying things I could never replace. Along with the list I'd left at the store was a note, which read something like this: 'Dear Storekeeper, I am in a jam and need supplies. Am sorry about the rifle, but I need that, too. I will look after it and you'll get it back for sure. The list of what I've taken is with the note, and the things will all be paid for some time. Very many thanks. Kurt Green.'

"My pockets were stuffed with meat and bread, and in one of them was the rest of the writing pad. I'd no need of it at the time, but some paper on which to keep track of the days would be useful, and another snack would save me unpacking my sack for a while. I had now left a definite clue for my pursuers to work on, and although I hoped the storekeeper would notice nothing amiss until morning, I knew I should have to travel fast in order to avoid being taken.

"With food inside me there was no reason why I should not travel throughout the night if there was enough light to show me the trail, and I set out for the west. The road was barely more than a wagon trail, but after a couple of hours the moon came up giving me enough light to show me that I was well into the foothills and that the mountains were not far ahead.

"Coming to some ranch buildings, the dogs kicked up a racket, so I backed up a little and waited until they quietened down. Making a wide detour, I came out well beyond the ranch house to find that the track was nothing more than a single packhorse trail. This was what I wanted. Here I could travel as fast or faster than the men who might come in search of me. In the dark horses would not be likely to move at more than walking pace, for mountain trails rarely lend themselves to a faster gait.

"It must have been after midnight when I heard the sound of an engine in the distance, and when it stopped I figured that the storekeeper and his wife had reached home. It was a dead still night and sounds travelled a

long way. An hour or two later I was confident that I was
well ahead of any possible pursuers, and I left the trail
prepared to have a rest. With the two blankets and the
slicker used half as a groundsheet and half on top to keep
off the dew, I was soon asleep.

" I awakened at dawn and looked back along the trail.
There was no sign of pursuers, and an inspection of the
trail proved no one had passed while I was asleep. A
trickle of water provided me with a drink, and I had a
sketchy sort of wash, though I did not wait to search my
sack for soap. The food in my pockets saved interfering
with my pack, and heading west with the minimum of
delay, I soon found myself in the mountains proper. From
time to time I paused at some vantage point to examine
the back trail, but apart from such halts I travelled fast
for some hours.

" About noon the valley in which I was travelling
ended in another running at right angles to it; that is,
north and south. Down it flowed a fair-sized creek, and
ahead of me was a high range. Here, I figured, was the
first check to my pursuers. I could step carefully, leaving
no tracks, and unless they had a dog they wouldn't know
which direction I had taken. Beyond that ridge there
would be another valley, and to reach a point opposite to
where I was in it by following a trail might mean a trip
of some fifty miles. If I could cross that ridge direct, I'd
be a day or more ahead of them.

" Going directly over the top would mean a tough trip
for five or ten miles, and I had to take the chance that I
could not make it at all. But the idea seemed worth
trying. First of all I went into the creek and waded up it
quite a way. Then I came out on to the trail, still leaving
no tracks that anyone but an Indian or a dog could follow.
Then I went back into the creek and about half way down
to the point where I had first entered it. This, I thought.
would fox even a dog for an hour or two.

" From this point I was to begin my attempt to cross
the ridge. Leaving the creek on the opposite side, I
" I set out early the next day, with an empty sack,

ST4*

well up and opposite the valley along which I first came, I found I could see the back trail in places for a good many miles. Here I stopped for a rest and a meal, water being provided by snow that lingered on the heights. I made a good meal and sorted out my stuff so that I could make a meal without disturbing everything I was carrying.

"It was too early in the season for there to be any tourists about. I might meet up with a trapper or prospector, but having been out of touch with the outside world for some time, he would not be suspicious.

"I wasn't acquainted with the country in which I found myself, but I had no special aim as to where I wanted to be as long as I was in the heart of the Rockies and off the beaten track. It was a tough climb with that heavy, awkward pack, all of two thousand feet above the valley floor. I took what looked like a pass, one of the lower gaps in the line of peaks, but making my way over the top of that ridge proved a longer job than I'd expected. The ridge extended a long way in both directions, and there were lots of ups and downs and detours before I came to a place from where I could see down into the valley at which I was aiming.

"It was getting on for sundown, and I still hadn't found a place where I could attempt to start down. Where I was the cliff was sheer for a couple of hundred feet, and I was about all in. But I didn't want to spend the night on the ridge. It would be chill, there was no water and nothing with which to make a fire. Away to my right was a fault which looked hopeful. A steeply sloping ledge led down to the main slope of the mountain. It was some thirty feet from the top of the cliff, but I felt it offered me a way down if only I could reach it.

"I let down my pack to a place where it would stay put, then looped my lariat round a point of rock. I let myself down, snaked the lariat free, and then, without anything worse than a few awkward stretches, got on to the slope. At the end of another half hour I was down in the valley. There was a large creek which I sure needed, for one thing I'd overlooked was something in which to carry water. I had a real wash, a good meal, and by the time I got around to a smoke darkness was falling. I'd noticed a trail threaded its way through the valley, but I was well away from that, and I felt pretty safe.

"I'd set myself the task of living alone in the Rockies, and I'd no idea how long I'd have to live by myself. It might be as much as a year or even longer. Luckily I'd enough food to last me a few weeks if I eked it out with some fish and a few spruce partridge.

"My first need was to find some inaccessible spot where I could make a permanent camp, live Indian style and prepare for a long, hard winter. I knew, of course, that the Indians had not been able to live on the country after they lost their prairies and the buffalo was wiped out. But I figured that where numbers failed to get by, one man might succeed. I'd been around with Indians quite a bit, and knew how they dried fish and game to preserve them. I also knew most of the herbs, berries and roots they used for medicines, fruit and vegetables. I'd seen them preparing these things, as well as buckskin, rawhide and what not, and we all know about Kinnick-Kinnick, the Indians' tobacco, which is not bad smoking once you get used to it.

"I reckoned then if I could find the right spot, I could collect and store enough grub and make some sort of shack before winter set in. With that in mind, I travelled north, then west, wherever possible keeping to valleys that led west. I hiked for about a week, never meeting a soul. Then I came to a big tree well blazed and with remnants of fire notices tacked to it. I knew that I was entering a National Park or a Forest Reserve. Now there was the risk of meeting up with a Warden out clearing trails, for the ones I'd seen hadn't been cleared.

"I didn't know this part of the country, but my luck did not desert me. Coming to another valley leading west I took the fork of the trail that went that way, and soon came to a clearing in which stood a cabin. It was the regular type of Warden's cabin, but there were no horses in the clearing and everything was still. Still, an hour passed before I went any nearer. Keeping in cover until I was nearly on top of it, I peeked in through the window.

" The blankets strung up on the roof and the general appearance of the place told me it had not been used since the previous summer. The Warden, I knew, might come any time, but I decided to risk a quick peep inside. The door wasn't locked, and I'd found what, for me, was better than a gold mine. There was a lot of food, much of it in good condition. There were pots and pans galore, and as many had not been used for years, I was sure they could be ' borrowed ' without being missed. An old map on the wall told me this was the south end of the Warden's district; that there was another cabin to the north at about twenty miles, his main cabin being about as far away again. The name 'Jim Thomas,' pencilled on the map made me think I'd discovered the name of the Warden.

" Even if he was on his way from the halfway cabin, it was so early that it would be a full hour before he arrived, and I set about making the most of my good fortune. The food left at the cabin by tourists the previous fall provided me with items I'd already used. The fire store by the cabin contained tools and kerosene, and that meant I might meet my needs from it in the future.

" I knew the food wouldn't be missed, and that it would only be thrown away if I didn't take it, and there seemed to be many items which could be borrowed without the Warden noticing. I decided that I needed a permanent camp within about twenty miles of the cabin. If my food showed signs of running out, then there were stocks here which would replenish it.

" The map told me that the trail I was on led to Porcupine Pass, and on the other side of that was British Columbia, which would be outside the warden's district. My search for permanent quarters had been narrowed a lot by finding the cabin. Taking care that I left no evidence of my visit, I set out for the foot of the pass.

There, having a good view of the back trail, I made camp, and felt very confident about my future.

"The next day I cached my pack, and set out light for the first time. Reaching the top of the pass, wild mountains stretched away before me as far as I could see. Apart from the Warden's cabins, and maybe a trapper's or prospector's shack, I felt sure there was no human habitation within a hundred miles. This was the region in which to hide up, but I still had to find a suitable spot. Leaving the trail, I came upon many possible places, but none that was just what I wanted.

"One site appealed to me more than any other. This was a spot surrounded with such a tangle of windfalls that anything larger than a fox would almost certainly miss it. Still, the place where I was to winter was too important to be chosen lightly, and I decided to give myself another two days of searching before making a final decision.

"And what a good thing I did. For the next day when I went to the top of the pass with the idea of making another trip in a different direction, I developed a hankering to climb to the summit of one of the peaks which guarded the pass. The climb was a hard one, but it proved to be more than worth while, for it led me to the very thing I wanted. The peak on which I was standing marked the end of a ridge, and I was sure it was a peak which had never been climbed before. It was not a mountain that the climbing enthusiast would have bothered about, and what had prompted me to haul myself up it I shall never know, but I've always had a feeling it was providence. For, a mile or so from where I was standing, the ridge divided, and there yawned a great cleft as if some giant had split it and pulled it apart lengthwise.

"Only from the peak on which I was standing could the cleft be seen, and it was one which no human being was likely to have seen before. I set out to investigate it with a feeling of excitement, and, three hours later, I knew I'd found the ideal retreat. The divide was about a mile long and three or four hundred yards wide in the middle. It tapered off at either end, and was so deep as to be below timber line. The floor, which was almost flat, was covered with a medium sized growth of spruce, and a thread of a creek ran through the centre. The sides were so steep as to be almost sheer, and at the far end was a small lake.

" A crack angled down the cliff which was used by goats and sheep, and it gave me right of way to the valley. I had found my ideal hiding place. The smoke from a camp fire would never be seen, and even the crack of a rifle would not be heard on the trail, for I was deep in solid rock. By using many different tracks when going in and out I would avoid making a trail, and I felt that I was no longer in danger of being caught even if they brought an army to comb the region.

" I made a bed and shelter of spruce boughs, and cooked a good meal, feeling as if I'd just achieved a victory. I had maybe five months before winter set in, plenty of time in which to do all that I had to do. The task appealed to me, and I felt real content."

IV: THE CRUSOE OF PORCUPINE PASS

WE HAD A MEAL. Then Dutch resumed his story.

"I cut a temporary trail to the far end of my little valley," he said, "to the lake which was fed by the creek. There was no outlet, so I guess the lake filled up and then seeped away underground. It was alive with fish, all about the same size of a pound apiece. I reckon they didn't get enough to eat to grow any bigger, as the water was greatly overcrowded. They were hungry all right, as they'd bite at anything, even taking a piece out of my finger if I stuck it in the water.

"I found herbs and berries that would be useful, and near the edge of the timber quite a plantation of kinnick-kinnick, so I was in no danger of running short of tobacco.

"My first job was to build myself a real cabin. For that I needed nails, a heavier axe, a spade and some wire, and my thoughts turned to the Warden's cabin. I could travel there and back in a day, and although it would be a long day it would be an odd journey now and then that would keep me trail hardened.

angled up the slope towards the mountains. When I was reaching the cabin inside six hours. There were no horses and I was pretty sure no one was around. But I took no chances until I'd made certain, and then I began collecting the things I needed. There were twenty-seven spades

in the store, and I was sure he wouldn't miss one out of
that lot. There were several heavy axes, too, and a bag of
nails tucked away in a corner. The bag was so old it was
falling in pieces, and wouldn't have been missed if I'd
taken the lot. But I took only what I knew I would need,
doing the same with the wire I found. I added to my
collection a larger frying pan than the one I'd taken from
the store and several clean cans from the garbage dump.
Topping the load off with a few more items of grub, I set
out for home, stopping a little way from the cabin to eat
a much needed meal. I was back in my hideout before
dark, having spent a very useful day.

" I started making the cabin first thing the next morning. Having cleared a level spot near the creek and cut a
set of poles, my home soon began to take shape. I
built a chimney with rocks, sealing it with clay from the
creek, a clay which set like rock when it got warm. In
the scree at the foot of the cliff were some rocks that split
into thin slabs when I hit 'em the right way. I made a
pole roof, covered it with my slabs and covered them with
sods to prevent them from slipping.

" My valley was well protected against wind, as it was
completely enclosed, but I knew plenty of snow would
blow in from the top and that the roof had to be strong
if my cabin was to remain dry. The building finished, I
made shelves, a table, a bunk, and a spruce mattress,
finishing them in ten days. Then I set to work on a dugout
where I could store fish and meat, which would get good
and cold in winter and act as a fridge well into summer.

" The only part of the cabin that set me a problem was
the window. I managed to make a door all right, but I
needed light in the place without having to keep the door
open all the time. I didn't quite solve the problem, but I
met it half way as it were by using some white paper in
which some of my goods had been wrapped. I greased it
with lard, and that made it more transparent and protected it when it got wet.

" With a home good enough for all I needed, I turned
my attention to the food supply. Going to the creek for

water one morning I found it full of fish. They were struggling in about two inches of water, trying to find a place to spawn. I caught a couple of dozen with my hands, and these started my fish reserve. Later I caught a lot more in the lake, and these I treated Indian fashion, half drying and half smoking them. They tasted as good as smoked salmon, and these I stored away, using fresh fish to help out the food. I meant to get more fish before the water froze solid, as I knew it would in winter, let them freeze, then store them in the dugout. By leaving it open a night or two it would get real frosted, and the warm days would not thaw it out.

"I then started in safeguarding my tobacco supply by getting hold of a lot of the plant and drying it. I started mixing it with the tobacco I still had left, for though I'd plenty of papers, I knew I should be smoking the Indian tobacco neat before winter set in. I decided to leave getting my meat until it was cold enough for it not to spoil.

"My chief trouble was the roots, berries and things that didn't grow in my valley. Expeditions were necessary to collect what I needed, and drying and storing them had me studying. But these problems had to be solved somehow, for I couldn't live on fish and meat without the danger of contracting scurvy.

"I made trips to find out just where the things I needed were most readily available, memorising their positions against the time they would be ready for gathering. Blueberries were ripe and I gathered and dried a lot of them. They did not look at all good, but the Indians said that, soaked and stewed, they were good for a man in winter. My flour reserve was dwindling and would soon be exhausted, and I had to find a substitute for vegetables. I gathered the roots I knew were eatable and dried them, but the storing of my growing food stocks presented a problem. I needed more containers, and the garbage dump at the Warden's cabin seemed better than trying to make pots with clay.

"I made another trip to the cabin, but this time the

Warden was in residence, and I hid up, deciding to wait
a while. I'd made no provision for an overnight stay, and
I was worried about my store of food. If a bear got at it
it would play havoc with my rations. Luckily, while I
was considering returning home and coming another day,
the Warden came out with a box of stuff, dumped it among
the garbage and then went back for more. On his third
trip into the open he carried a halter, and having caught
his horses he tied them to the hitch rail.

"It was evident that he was about to leave and that
the way would be clear for me within a few minutes. He
was middle-aged and genial looking, and although I was
never troubled with being lonesome he was the first
human being I had seen in weeks, and I would have
appreciated a word with him. That being impossible, I
kept hid up while he made ready to leave.

"As soon as he was out of sight I went to the garbage
dump. In addition to the cans I needed, I found the
Warden had dumped most of the grub which had been in
the cabin, amongst it the best part of a twenty-five pound
sack of flour. Although the flour was a bit lumpy round
the edges, the find was a valuable one. So, too, was the
large can of coffee I found there. It was a little stale maybe, but it was far better than no coffee at all. I found
other items which I could use, and took home a very
valuable haul.

"My anxiety about a bear visiting my place in my
absence caused me to put out a few dried fish where
they would draw his attention away from the cabin and
the dugout, and to one I fastened a string and attached
the other end to my 'rifle, so that it would go off when the
fish was taken. I'd no wish to kill the bear, although the
gun might do so by chance; but the explosion would
frighten him so badly he would be unlikely to trespass on
my preserves again.

"During the summer I made several longish trips
collecting roots and herbs, and during the tourist season
I had to leave the trail at times to allow the sightseers
to pass. I brought myself somewhat up to date with what

was happening in the world outside when I came upon a newspaper left at a camping site. It was only a fortnight old, and I read every word of it, including the ads. It made no mention of an escaped prisoner, and judging by the situation in Europe the war showed no sign of being over before winter.

" On my travels I happened upon the stamping ground of a young bull moose over in the B.C. region, and I earmarked him for myself when the time was opportune. I also found places frequented by deer and there was an elk on the park side. I was anxious not to have to shoot the elk, however, preferring to get my meat in B.C. Although unaware of the fact, the Warden had been a great help to me, and I resolved to shoot game in his district only as a last resource.

" By early fall I was almost ready for the winter. I had stored all my berries, roots and leaves, and I had an ample supply of Indian tobacco. I had some cans cleaned ready for storing fat when I killed my meat, and I had made myself snowshoes which only needed the rawhide and which would be to hand when I shot an elk or the moose I had promised myself.

" That moose came to mind in October when I heard some shots from over in B.C. It was not a game preserve as was the Park, and I hoped it was not my moose which had fallen to the shooting.

" According to my calendar it was near the end of October, though I may have missed a day or two from my pad. As winter would be starting any time there was little likelihood of any shooting parties being left in the Reserve, and certainly there would be no tourists. The nights were becoming pretty cold, and although snow might still be a month away, I couldn't be sure, and I was hankering to make sure of my meat. So I went to the Warden's cabin to see if he had packed up for the winter, knowing that all parties would be out of the district if he had gone.

" The weather was wonderful, the air having a sparkle with it, and I enjoyed the hike. The blankets and mattress on the bunk had been rolled up and slung to the roof. The place was tidy, logs and kindling were stacked by the stove and everything indicated that the Warden had gone. A note on the table drew my attention. It read: ' Dear Mr Spencer, I expected your party to be here before now, but there's nothing to keep me down at this end and you'll find me at the main cabin, and will see you there.' It was signed: *Jim Thomas, Warden.*

" The Warden had gone all right, but it seemed he had pulled out only that morning or perhaps the day before. And the note made it clear that there was a shooting party in the neighbourhood and liable to visit the cabin at any moment. This was not the time to relax, and a few minutes later I was glad I'd read that note. For I was sorting out a few cans from the garbage heap when I heard voices from the direction of Porcupine Pass. This could only be the hunting party, and I was well hidden in the bush when they came into sight. There was the guide, a couple of dudes and a horse wrangler-cook. They had half a dozen pack horses and from the packs jutted heads of game in plenty. The party had had a successful trip. They made ready for lunch, and it was while they were having it that I heard a snatch of talk that made me prick up my ears.

" It's a pity about that grub in the Porcupine cabin," the guide said. " As the Warden's not coming back it seems the pack rats will get it all. If the Warden didn't want it he might have put a wandering family of Indians on to it."

" It can't be helped," one of the party replied. " Better leave the grub behind than the moose."

So they might have got my bull moose. But my thoughts were on that cabin on Porcupine Creek where, it seemed, there was a large store of food. The cabin would be somewhere down the trail, though how far I could only guess. Dudes travel no more than twenty miles a day as a rule, but for all that the cabin might be anything up to fifty miles away. But it contained food, and I had to find it before the pack rats got busy.

" On returning to my cabin I found I'd had a visitor in my absence. Some of the fish were gone and the rifle had been fired, and bear tracks in the mud near the creek were the visiting card I was looking for. Having exploded the rifle, I wasn't expecting the bear to return, but he proved to be a venturesome beast. After supper, he came prowling round the cabin again, and although I wasn't fond of bear meat, the hide and fat would be useful to me. Besides, although bears would soon be holing up for the winter, I couldn't afford to have one rifling my food in my absence.

" A black bear weighing some six hundred pounds, I got him between the eyes with my first shot, but I'd no time to deal with him. My first task was to find Porcupine cabin, and I was sure the bear would keep for a day or two, particularly as there seemed to be no coyotes in my valley.

" I set off early next morning with sufficient items to make a rough camp if that proved necessary. The tracks left by the string of horses were easy to follow, but I was over the pass and some twenty miles beyond it and still there was no sign of the cabin. I made camp for the night, being some thirty-five miles from the Warden's cabin, and thinking I had at least another ten miles before reaching my destination.

" The next morning, however, I'd gone only a few miles when I realised that there were no longer horse tracks on the trail. Retracing my steps for a few yards I came upon a side track winding into the bush and knew I had found Porcupine cabin. It was an old tumbledown shack beside Porcupine Creek, built years before by a prospector who had sunk a bit of a shaft there.

" What I found in the cabin, however, was of more value to me than any gold. There was the best part of fifty pounds of flour, twenty pounds of rolled oats, as much sugar, an unopened ten pound can of lard, coffee, tea, half a side of bacon, a couple of dozen cans of assorted goods, candles, and other things besides.

" It took me two days to pack all I could carry of the

stuff back to my hideout. All the canned goods and other things I thought could be safely left I cached in the old mine shaft, where it would be safe until I was ready to fetch it.

"That trip persuaded me that I had to make a proper packboard with a tump line, for the old sack hung low and dug into my back, tiring me far more than was necessary. Having dealt with the bear, I made a packboard, and that was the position when I had my first fall of snow. According to my reckoning, this took place on the tenth of November, and although the fall was light, and not more than six inches, it announced the definite arrival of winter. The temperature at nights was slumping to around zero, and I knew that I was facing my most critical period and that it was bound to last for a long time. I couldn't afford an accident, for with no one to help me it was more than likely to prove fatal, and I couldn't afford to run short of food. In the valley the days were cold and short, for the sun was low and not much of it found its way between the high ridges.

"I left the dugout open for a night or two and the inside of it was like a fridge. Then I caught more fish, froze them solid and stored them, confident they would be in perfect condition when the time came to eat them. Then I went after my moose, getting him the first day, the snow making it easy for me to follow his tracks. It took me the best part of a week to hump him home, the hide alone making a good load, but I had meat for the winter, and enough perhaps to make it unnecessary for me to eat bear meat. The skin was a bit heavy for rawhide, but I put some strips in soak right away.

"I was watching the weather pretty closely, for I had no snowshoes, and I'd no wish to be caught far from home in a blizzard. The rest of the hide I stretched for making buckskin. My clothes would not wear for ever and were not suitable for severe cold, and unless I could do something about a suitable wardrobe I was in danger of being a prisoner in my cabin for something like six months.

"With my moose safely home, I set to work on my buckskin, but the Indians knew more about these things than I did. Though I worked plenty of bear grease into it, it remained too stiff for the use I wanted to make of it. Still I managed to make a fair pair of shoepacs which came over my mocassins to about halfway up my legs. My rawhide was as hard as iron and difficult to work, but I managed to string my snowshoes with it. The hide, however, dried out as taut as strings in a tennis racket, and it was not only rough but was by no means as light as I had hoped. Still it was strong and would serve my purpose well enough.

"Winter proper came at the end of November with a blizzard that lasted four days. Although the wind couldn't force its way into my valley, the snow was deep, and large quantities were blown down from the top of the ridge. There were bound to be drifts that were very deep, for the average fall was around five feet.

"Then the bottom fell out of the temperature, and I was right up against it, my resources being tested with more than fifty degrees below zero. I was snug enough in the cabin, which was so buried that I had to clear a place for light to get in at the window. I had plenty of fuel, too, and was quite safe in my cabin, but I had no intention of staying there. Having given the snow a couple of days in which to settle, I tried out my shoes. They worked fine, but I did not go far. For one thing I'd no wish to develop severe snowshoe pains by being too eager, and for another the cold was more than a match for my clothes. I put on all the underwear that I had, and tried wrapping the bear hide round me. But the skin wasn't properly dressed and was too heavy and awkward, and although it served well as a top cover to my bed it was no use as clothing. Nevertheless, I'd no intention of staying in my cabin. I had to have exercise and interests, and I had to have the rest of the grub from Porcupine cabin. Besides, there were a lamp and some kerosene at the Warden's place, and I was determined to have those as well.

ST5

"I hardened up my legs with a few short trips, and as soon as the cold let up a little I set out for the Warden's cabin. My packboard proved a great success. It sat well on my back, there were no lumps, and I could ease off the pull on my shoulders with the tump line.

"There were no tracks other than those made by game, and I made good time to the cabin. I filled a half empty can of kerosene up with a little from each of the other cans, knowing four gallons would last me a long time. Then I turned my attention to the large bundle of blankets stored in case of fire. As the outside blanket looked faded and dusty it seemed they had not been opened for a long time. Unrolling the bundle, I took out half a dozen, and when the remainder were done up again they looked much the same as before. After a meal, I was on my way home again, complete with lamp, kerosene and blankets. But I decided not to visit the place again until spring. I could not help leaving obvious tracks, and it was just possible that the Warden would make a trip on the lookout for fur poachers.

"The blankets were nothing like as good as the Hudson Bay type I had brought from the store, but there were more of them and they would serve well as bedclothes. Although I didn't like doing it, I cut up the two good blankets and made a fine parka and pair of over pants. I strung the wrists and ankles to keep out the snow, did the same with the hood and neck, and had an outfit in which to face almost any weather. Not that they looked anything like tailor made, but they were strictly utility and they served well the purpose for which I'd made them.

"Although I had some woollen and leather mitts I'd brought with me, I used some of the blanket I had left over to make a couple of hand muffs which I strung together to carry round my neck. Protected from the cold in this way, I hiked around quite a bit, got the rest of the grub from Porcupine cabin, and felt I'd done all I could to face the winter. Naturally everything I did took a deuce of a long time, but time was the one thing I had in plenty.

"Come what I figured was Christmas Day I couldn't have fed better no matter where I'd been. There was a spruce partridge I'd caught in the fall with the old bent springy stick and fishing line method, and with this I ate canned peas and carrots. I followed with a can of peaches and evaporated milk, and finished with coffee and a cigarette of real tobacco. The last luxury proved less satisfying than I'd thought, for I'd got so used to Indian tobacco that I almost preferred it.

"Although I still had a few luxuries left which I'd brought from Porcupine Creek, I used them very sparingly after my extravagant Christmas Day celebrations. The time passed, and the sun began to stay longer above the ridge. Some days, in fact, it was quite warm, but there were more blizzards and cold spells, and by constantly replenishing my woodpile I had no difficulty keeping warm indoors. The fire never went out, and I hardly used a match all winter.

"With the arrival of spring the snow began to go. I had kept the dugout clear to make sure that it kept real cold, and in the late spring I still had fish and meat in good condition. Having survived the winter, I looked forward to summer with some confidence. To my surprise, though, my luck seemed to have petered out, and I fed less hearty than I had done during the winter. The Warden's cabin and a few camp sites provided a few odds and ends, but I had no good hauls as in the summer before. You can tell how things were with me when I say that I found a couple of loaves of bread at a camp site that were going a bit mouldy. Yet I ate them as if they were the most delicious meal that ever came my way.

"There's no need to go over that summer and the winter that followed it. I returned the Warden's lamp in good time and borrowed it again for the next winter. But it was a tough year. I collected enough meat and Indian stuff for the winter, but I was without flour, coffee and all the good things, and I lived in real Indian style, minus, of course, the buffalo steaks they used to get and without the knack of doing things in the excellent way the squaws knew how to do them.

"Flour was the thing I missed most of all. If I'd been able to make a bannock or biscuits to eat with my meat and root stews, then I'd have been really satisfied. Still, although my meals lacked variety, I kept healthy and never once got real hungry.

"The few old newspapers I came across told me the war was still on, and showed no sign of ending. Came the third summer, and it proved little better than the first. I lived mostly on fish, spruce partridge, rabbits, roots and berries, of which I'd collected a large stock.

"In 1918 I spent the fourth summer in the wilds, and my luck was in again. One day, having wandered farther afield than ever before, I came upon a large open place south of Porcupine Creek. It was larger than those usually encountered in these mountains, and there was a big slough covered with tall grass at the edges and alive with water birds of all kinds.

"Trapping the birds would have been easy, but it would have been useless, for they would have spoiled, and I was more interested in what they were eating. They were feeding on something growing on what looked like tall grass, and I noticed that seeds shucked out as they pushed their way through. And the seed, whatever it was, seemed to be good, judging by the way the birds were diving their heads into the water and the eagerness with which they were eating it.

"When I got near enough to examine the seed I saw that it was wild rice. I'd heard that it grew in the big sloughs out on the prairies, and remembered reading that the Indians used it the way we use wheat, in the old days. In fact, it looked very much like third grade wheat, and I saw in it something that might serve as a good substitute for flour. At least I could boil it and make some sort of porridge, while there was a chance I'd find a way to grind it and make biscuits.

"I lay my slicker on the water with the edges propped up by the reeds and shook the rice over it. I got about a

quarter of a pound as a reward for my efforts, but found
that a great deal of the seed did not fall off. So I bent a
good armful over the slicker and beat it with a stick. I got
plenty of chaff that way, but a good pound of rice as well.
In this way I knew I would soon have a load, and as I
always carried my sack with me wherever I went, I
emptied it of my camping stuff and half filled it with rice.
This, along with my camping equipment, was as much
as I could carry, for I was a long way from home.

"I boiled some of it and it swelled up and tasted good.
I found a quick way of separating the husks by shaking
up a small quantity in my slicker and fanning it. I ground
some of it with a flat stone and the head of my axe, and
although this proved to be a tedious process I got a kind
of flour. If there's nothing else left behind at a camp,
there's always a quantity of baking powder, and I had a
plentiful supply. By adding the baking powder to the
ground rice I made some very tasty biscuits.

"Not long afterwards I had a much greater stroke of
luck. I was after more rice, and on my way down Porcupine Creek, when I came upon a copy of a newspaper of
fairly recent date. It contained little of genuine interest,
but it was a local paper and one item caught my eye, for
it related to Porcupine Creek. The article stated that oil
drilling on the Porcupine Creek well was to be discontinued at once. There was little chance of getting oil
before winter, and operations were well nigh impossible
during winter due to transport difficulties. The company
being confident of ultimate success, however, the well
was not being entirely abandoned.

"Obviously an outfit of that kind always left behind a
whole heap of things, especially when it was expensive to
take out items which they had spent a lot of money bringing in. It was rarely economical to remove such things as
flour, and if the outfit was a big one, as the newspaper
suggested, then if I could only find the oil drillings I
would be well provided for throughout the winter. That,
though, was the problem, for I'd no means of knowing
where the oil well might be. A creek can go a long

way before finally joining up with a river, and there were other Porcupine Creeks besides the one where I was.

"The town in which the paper was published suggested that I was on the right creek, and I determined to make a thorough search. Having brought to my cabin another load of rice, I got together enough grub to last me several days and started off down the creek. Three days hiking found me sixty miles from the pass and the creek had become quite a large stream. But the trail continued without showing any sign of an oil well, and my position was becoming precarious. It was the hunting season, and I had to take cover a few times to avoid shooting parties. I dare not go on for more than another half day, for my food supplies were down to the minimum, and I would be half starved before I could return to my cabin.

"I was on the verge of quitting, and was trying to reassure myself that I would face the winter with my supplies enlarged by more wild rice, when I climbed what I had decided must be my last rise in the trail. Had I drawn a blank then, I was determined to turn back. But there, only a short way ahead, was the thing I had come so far to find. An oil derrick!

"The place proved to be deserted and was quite a fair set-up. There were several buildings made of local timber and others made of prepared lumber which had been packed in on horses. There were shacks, a store, a kitchen, an office and bunkhouse.

"The store had been cleaned out, but not the cookhouse. None of the sacks, cartons or tins which had been opened had been removed. There were at least eighty pounds of flour, and supplies of practically everything that I needed. Had I left it someone else less in need than I was would have taken it, or else it would have spoiled. I sorted out as large a collection as I could manage, and sought a cache that neither humans nor animals were likely to find. A padlock with a key hanging on the wall of the office solved the problem. Into the office went the rest of the goods, the door was locked, the key hidden, and I had the safest cache possible.

" Before leaving I looked into the other building which proved to be a bunkhouse. There I found an old mackinaw jacket and pants, socks, underwear and over-alls. Normally I might have thrown such things away, seeing the state they were in, but to me they were more precious than all the oil the company hoped to find. All the things needed was a wash. A box under a bunk was half full of soap, something I'd been without for more than a year. I also collected a pile of magazines, which I hoped I might hump to my cabin one day after I'd moved all the grub. But a trip to this place in winter would take a week or more, and I'd not be able to take a full load. I'd have to carry equipment to see me safely through a blizzard, and that meant plenty of blankets and the slicker.

" I looked in a mirror hanging on the wall and got a shock. I knew I'd a good beard and that my hair was long, but I hadn't bargained for the wild man of the woods who gazed back at me from that glass. One thing I'd over-looked was a razor, and I decided I'd have to do some-thing to reduce my growth on head and face before showing myself, however distant that event might be.

" That winter proved to be a good one for me. I made several trips to the oil well, and it was always tough going. Once, in fact, I thought I wasn't going to make it. On the way there I had to hole up because of a blizzard. I nearly ran out of food, and I came very near to freezing to death. Even when the blizzard let up and I was able to get going again, the snow was that soft it was as much as I could do to make ten miles a day. Still, I made out, and got everything finally, including the magazines. I was now quite used to being alone, and those magazines proved to be good company. So much so that I read every one of 'em through two or three times.

" It was in the early summer of 1919 that I learnt that the war was over. The first paper I saw that year was

one the Warden left in his cabin. The war was over, but
I didn't know whether I shouldn't be clapped into gaol
if I showed up and announced who I was. And I was
taking no chances. After thinking the position over, I
decided to approach the Warden. Yet I had no wish to go
to his cabin. I had the feeling that it would be better if
I met him more on my own ground, although why it
should be that way I couldn't make out.

"He was usually at the cabin at this time of the year
about once a week, and he generally rode up the pass
before leaving. I knew I was a sight with my makeshift
clothing, long hair and beard, but when I tried trimming
my beard with my hunting knife I found I was only
making it look worse, so gave up. Looking at myself in
the bottom of a can, which was all I had for a mirror, I
saw I was liable to scare the Warden to death.

"I camped out near the pass waiting for him, and I
didn't have to wait long. On the third afternoon I heard
a single horse approaching on the trail. This, I knew,
would be him, and I felt a bit queer. I hadn't spoken to a
soul for over three years, and hardly knew how to go
about it.

"The Warden dismounted at the pass, sat on a rock

and lit a cigarette. His horse pricked its ears as I started to move.

" 'What can you see, feller?' said the Warden. 'Bear or somethin'?'

" He looked the way the horse was looking, and that was where I was coming out of the bush as nonchalantly as I could.

" 'Good afternoon,' I blurted out.

" He was an elderly man with a grizzled, kindly face, and piercing blue eyes. He was appraising me keenly, taking in every detail, and as he did not speak, I said: 'My name's Kurt Green. Some call me Dutch.'

" 'Wal,' he drawled, 'I don't know where you sprung from, young feller, but wherever it is you seem to have been there a hell of a long time.'

" I laughed, knowing I looked part Indian, part wild man and maybe even part bear.

" 'Is your name Thomas, Warden?' I asked. 'I've seen it on the map in your cabin.'

" 'It is,' he said.

" 'I've seen you lots of times,' I told him, 'and I feel I know you quite well. I've been around here quite a while. You see, I was determined not to get drafted, and lit out. I've just found out the war is over, and I'd like to discuss a few things with you.'

" 'I'll be everlastingly hornswoggled,' the Warden said. 'I've never heard the like of it. You mean you've hid out here some place for as long as two or three years?' He seemed to find that amusing. 'Excuse my mirth,' he said, 'but it strikes me as funny you dodging the Army and doing it such a hard way. Then not even knowing the war is over!' He slapped his thigh and roared with laughter.

" 'You come right down to my cabin,' he decided, 'and tell me all about it.'

" 'But didn't you never hear of me?' I asked. 'Did you never learn of my escape from the hoosegow?'

" 'Never heard of you before, son,' he said. 'Do you know where my cabin is?'

" 'I do. I've been there many times to see what you'd thrown out. And I borrowed some things you hadn't thrown out.'

" 'Wonders will never cease,' he chuckled. 'You must stay overnight and tell me all about it. There's plenty of blankets.'

" 'Not as many as you think, Mr Thomas,' I told him. 'I've borrowed some, but—'

"He laughed fit to burst.

" 'And eaten a deer or two I'm supposed to look after, I'll bet,' he said. And then he laughed some more.

" 'One deer and one bear, Warden,' I admitted. 'But all my other meat came from B.C.'

"I told the Warden my story and how I'd helped myself to things from his cabin, promising him everything would be returned except the food and kerosene.

" 'You're sure welcome to the grub,' he said. 'I never missed a thing. I guess you know better than me how many tools and blankets there should be. I ain't had a check up this three or four years.'

"I showed him my hideout, and he was tickled with it. He had no idea such a place existed, and he promptly named it Green Pasture. Before leaving for his headquarters he cut my hair and gave me a razor to make myself presentable. He promised to find out what the position was, and to bring me some clothes which I could pay for when I got back on my feet. He was a friendly feller, and it struck me he would most likely have kept my secret had I met him long before. He was paying a visit to town and promised to be back within a couple of weeks. Meanwhile, if I was short of anything I was to help myself at the cabin.

"He came back with a whole outfit of clothing, and brought in extra grub, including fresh bread and fruit, potatoes and other things I hadn't tasted for years. He'd made what enquiries he could, and he was certain that all I had to do was go out, find a job and keep quiet.

" 'Then no one will be any the wiser,' he said.

"I was grateful all right to Jim Thomas, and I kept

in touch with him until he retired. Naturally I paid him what I owed him as soon as I'd scraped the money together.

"I went out to the north, got a job as a horse wrangler where I was little known, and the folk thought I'd returned from the Army. Only my brothers and a few neighbours back home knew the truth, and my secret was safe with them.

"When my father died I got my share of the farm and bought my present outfit, but before that happened I'd saved up about two hundred dollars, enough to square up the storekeeper from whom I'd taken so much the day I left gaol. All I knew was that the place was called North Fork, which only meant that it was on the north fork of some creek. But a map and my memory helped me to trace back my journey, and I borrowed the Boss's car and drove out there.

"Reaching the store, I went in by the *front* door and a man came from the back room. I didn't recognise him, only having seen him from a distance, so I said: 'Remember anyone with the name of Kurt Green?'

"'No, can't say as I do,' he replied. 'But Green's a fairly common name. Did he live around here?'

"'No,' I said. 'But he was here a few years ago for a short time. Maybe you wasn't here then?'

"'Well, I've been here twenty-five years come spring,' he said.

"Satisfied that this was my man, I said: 'Maybe you remember a feller named Green who came here some years ago when you were away in town. He took some supplies and left a list of what he'd taken.'

"'Oh, that Green!' he exclaimed. 'What do you know about him?'

"'I'm that Green,' I said. 'And I've come to pay the bill.'

"He grinned. 'I knew you'd come,' he said. Then he shouted, 'Lois, come here!'

"His wife came into the store and he told her who I was and the reason for my visit.

" ' I guess we'd almost forgotten about it,' she smiled. ' But we always knew you'd come back some day. You must stay and eat.'

" Then I showed them the rifle, offering either to buy it or pay rent on it, whichever he wished.

" ' You'll do neither,' he said. ' I set some store on that gun and I'm right glad to get it back. You needed it and you were welcome to it.'

" Over the meal they told me that the police had never contacted them, and they had never heard of Dutch Green or his escape. They didn't ask why I was on the run, and when I told them they said that it was none of their business. As for the things I'd taken, apart from the rifle, blankets and one or two other items, they'd never have known what had gone had I not left the list. And they figured that, as I'd taken the trouble to make the list, I certainly didn't mean to steal anything.

" But the list could not be found, and those good folk said it didn't matter, anyway, after all this time. But I remembered that, except for the rifle, the stuff I'd had would be worth around eighty-five dollars, and I made them take a hundred to make up the interest on the loan."

All the time Dutch had been talking I'd been picturing his hideout in Green Pasture. It needed courage to live out three full winters in the wilds without any certainty of supplies other than those which came to hand. Dutch hadn't quite had to live on the country, and he would have had a lean time if he'd been compelled to do so. Other men hid up in the Rockies to avoid being drafted, and some men have taken to the bush, thinking they could live in the wilds. Most of the draft dodgers didn't last very long, and even those who went to live in the bush prepared for the life, gave it up after a few months at most. But Dutch Green, on the run, had little opportunity at the beginning to collect the things he needed. Fortune favoured him highly when he was able to secure so much food and equipment at the outset from the store at North Fork. Nevertheless, it was slender enough, and was only a fraction of what he would have got together had he been given the time and opportunity to buy at leisure what he needed.

He was lucky, too, in being able to make such use of the things at the Warden's cabin and in the various finds he made. Nevertheless, on very meagre resources he braved nearly four years in the wilds, including three full winters, with their blizzards, snowdrifts and savage frosts. His diet for months on end must have been exceedingly monotonous, and the lack of human fellowship would have caused many to lose their reason.

Dutch, however, came through unhurt in mind and sound in body. I saw him several times after he had told me his story, and then he went to live in the States. And Dutch, not being a writing man, slipped out of my life and I never heard of him again.

V : WINTER FARE

USUALLY, like other Forest Rangers, I left the Rockies
before the onset of winter, but this year I was asked to
stay on. Not to do my normal work, for when the snow
and frost take over everything comes to a halt. There are
no visitors or hunters, and while poachers might make
their way in, they are rare, and the Rangers keep a watch
for them in the spring or summer when they are on their
way out.

The Government, however, was anxious to check the
flow of the streams and rivers in the Sikanaska region
during the winter months, and I was detailed to undertake the work. Measuring the flow had given me an extra
job throughout the summer, and had taken but little of
my time. In winter, however, the task is a very different
matter. The smaller creeks are solid ice, the river over-
flows and freezes several times, piling up ice to a depth
of several feet, and the work is carried out at times in
over sixty degrees of frost, or worse.

The normal procedure is to take measurements at
different depths in three places; in the centre of the river
and about a third of the distance from each bank. The
little torpedo-like instrument with which the flow of
water is checked is connected to an earphone and a small

battery. As the propeller revolves a ticking is heard which is timed against a stop watch. Thus, by referring to a rather complicated table of figures it is possible to ascertain the number of cubic feet of water passing a given point each minute.

In mid-winter, when the flow of the creeks is very slight and there is little water passing down the sides of the river, only one measurement is taken in the river's centre at a couple of different depths. As the journey to and from the river may involve a battle against snow and bitter winds, a winter measurement often took a whole day.

For such work, little provision can be made to safeguard the Ranger who undertakes it. He is cut off from the outside world, for the telephone is almost certain to be out of order and all the passes are choked to a depth of many feet, the snow closing them at the first fall and making them impassable for weeks on end.

I had not, however, to face the difficulties that beset Dutch Green. I had ample provisions of every kind, plus the clothes designed to protect me against the most fierce and prolonged spell of cold. My cabin was stout and fuel was plentiful, and I was equipped with snowshoes and had nothing to fear from the weather, if I exercised care.

My readings of the meter which was submerged in the river were usually a simple matter, but I encountered difficulty when the meter developed the curious habit of ceasing to register for a few seconds. The earphone also emitted sounds very much like those produced on the radio by atmospherics, and I was compelled to begin my measuring of the water again. This interruption, however, kept recurring, and though I examined the instrument most carefully I could find nothing wrong with it.

Making a hole in ice several feet thick is not an easy task, and on this particular day I encountered more trouble than usual. The water had been flooding over the ice and there was no sign of the hole I had used previously. For cutting the ice I used a large steel ice chisel and this I kept stuck in the snow near the scene of operations. It had a handle six feet long and was fairly heavy.

Locating the site of my former excavation, I was not long getting through the top ice which was some six inches deep. But before the river had flooded and filled the hole, some two feet of ice had formed under about three feet of water. This made things very awkward, as it was exceedingly cold. As soon as I brought the wet chisel out of the water to make another cut it coated with ice. Thus the chisel became heavier and heavier, until I had to stop and break the ice off. My attacks on the ice below the water had resulted in a great deal of splashing, and my clothes were covered with icicles. More dangerous was the state of my mocassins. They anchored me to the ice, and great care had to be taken in freeing them, or they would have been torn to shreds. Thus the job was lengthy, tedious and not without a certain amount of risk.

With sufficient room at last to get the meter down I was taking the first measurement when, by some freak of reflection due to the position of the sun and the shape of the hole, a bright beam of light shone right down to the rocks on the bottom of the river. As the water was well up the sides of the hole and, in consequence, still, the swift current did not obscure the view, and I could see the little torpedo, its propeller spinning merrily.

It was then that I saw what had been interfering with my measuring of the flow of water. For there was a flash of silver and a fish, not much larger than the meter, attacked and did its best to swallow it.

Aware of the cause of the trouble, I took a hook and spinner with me on my next visit to the hole. But the trout made no move to bite, nor did they on the several occasions when I took my line. Neither the lure nor the meter was attacked. But the first time I left my fishing tackle at the cabin the trout got busy on the torpedo again.

Hanging on the wall of the cabin at Wind Lake was a pair of skis. I used these from time to time, but only for short expeditions, as the trails twisted and turned amongst trees and snowshoes were much more serviceable. Also there were times when the skis would not slide, and there were others when they moved only too easily. Not being an expert skier and finding the downhill slopes tempted me to an excessive speed, I decided that for all practical purposes the skis had better remain on the cabin wall. To be made helpless on the trail by a broken leg or ankle could only have one outcome.

On the slope of the mountain behind the cabin, however, was a large clear space, and half way from its summit was a drop of some twenty feet, then a stretch that was almost level. As winter continued I had rather a lot of time on my hands, and the skis and slope beckoned more and more. Eventually I yielded to the temptation, very nearly paying for my temerity with my life. For the slope was much too steep for the uninitiated, and had I not heard a story from a Swiss guide and acted upon what I learnt from it I should certainly have died.

The guide used to bring climbing parties out to Sikanaska in the summer. Some years before, he told me, a party of three had gone from Banff for a day's skiing, and decided they could dispense with the services of a guide. They were warned not to use a certain slope as it was notorious for avalanches, but they either misunderstood the instructions or thought it safe to ignore them. In any case, they essayed the slope, with the result that they were buried in a big snow slide. Failing to return, a search party was sent out led by the Swiss guide. Helped by lanterns and torches, they soon reached the scene of the disaster. A ski sticking out of the snow revealed the whereabouts of the skiers. Two were alive though unconscious and one had a broken leg. Of the third, however, there was no sign, and the search had to be abandoned until daylight. But further efforts to locate the missing man proved fruitless, although the other two claimed they had all three been together when the

ST6

avalanche of snow caught them. Hundreds of tons of snow were shifted right down to the bare rock, but the third member was not found.

A further search was made when the snow began to melt and the body was found a hundred and fifty feet from the spot where the other two skiers had been found. The poignant truth was that the hapless skier had burrowed through the snow all that way, changing direction several times, but without managing to come to the surface. In fact, in places he had gone deeper into the snow. Had his energies been directed to making an upward movement he would have covered but a fraction of the distance before pushing through into the open. As it was he had clawed away the snow until exhaustion and suffocation overcame him.

The guide, who had had experience of such things in Switzerland, said that there is a lot of air in the churned up snow of an avalanche, and sufficient to keep a man alive quite some time if he stays in one place. Providing he is uninjured and does not panic, he can burrow his way out, obtaining fresh supplies of air as he goes. If he panics, however, he is lost.

The story was simply a story to me until I ventured on that slope behind the cabin. At first all went well. I had several exhilarating trips, and became so expert in managing the skis that I could zigzag down and shoot over the twenty foot drop, keeping on my feet almost every time. The sport seemed safe enough, as I was near the cabin, and it gave me some much needed exercise.

Above where I began my run down was a wall of rock that was almost perpendicular, and I was making my way up when the large drift of snow piled against it began to slip. The snow beneath me rose higher and higher in a gigantic wave, under the thrust of the weight from above, and then it broke and went rushing down the slope with a lot more from higher up tumbling after it. The Swiss guide had told me that a man on skis could ride a snow slide, but I wasn't that kind of a skier.

I pitched head first into the moving mass, being bowled

over as if by a big wave breaking near the shore. I was
in the dark, my nose and mouth were full of snow, and,
although I experienced no great pressure and felt no
pain, I was being rolled over and over.

After what seemed a very long time all became still,
and in the pitch black I could feel a weight of snow
pressing on me. Being naturally inclined to claustro-
phobia, I began to panic. Being buried alive induced the
most terrible sensation, and I frantically clawed a space
around my face and spat out the snow. I could breathe,
and I remembered the guide's warning that to give way
to terror could only be fatal.

I forced myself into a state of greater calmness,
although I was still on the edge of panic, and took stock
of my position. One leg was so heavily weighted that it
would not move. Drawing up the other, I forced the
comparatively loose snow away with my hands and free
leg and provided myself with space enough for movement.

The air supply seemed to be adequate, but terror nearly
overwhelmed me, and I had to fight it down several times.
I managed to double up and reach my other leg, which
was anchored to its ski. Loosening it, I was then in a
position to enlarge the hole. But I realised that the snow
was harder to push away. It was settling down rapidly,
although my little cave still remained intact.

Until now I had little idea which was up, down or
sideways. Keeping still, however, I felt the weight on my
right side, and so decided that up was roughly to the left.
By now I had pretty well conquered the surges of panic,
and I started to study which would be the nearest way
to the open air.

The snow above me would still be inclined, and the
nearest way out would probably be away from the mountain, and at an angle. But which way? It was impossible
to tell. And again, in going up I must be sure of going
straight, otherwise, if the slope was steep, as it was almost
certain to be, I could go on moving parallel to the incline
without ever breaking through into the open.

ST6*

Taking out a match, I dried a thumbnail by rubbing it vigorously on my coat, and struck the match on it. My cave was too small for me to sit up, and panic asserted itself again, but only for a moment. For I noticed the flame of the match was not straight up. It was, of course, but not in the direction I had thought "up" to be. In fact, it was a good thirty degrees out of line with my ideas. Thinking a current of air might be acting on it, I decided I must make sure before using any more energy. For, whether it was my imagination or not, the air seemed to be giving out.

In my pocket was a bootlace and my metal matchbox kept against emergencies. In the darkness I tied the box to the bootlace to make an improvised plumb line. Striking another match I saw that the line agreed with the flame of the lucifer. Scratching a fair-sized hole at the top of the plumb line to serve as a guide, I returned the box and bootlace to my pocket and started to claw down the roof.

As the snow fell around me I was able to get to my knees, enlarging the hole as I went. The snow sank considerably as I pounded it with my knees, and I was able to stand up. I pulled down a lot more snow from around me until a heap formed underneath and I rose to the top of my burrow. When my cave was left below, I cleared enough room to get out the plumb line and a match. But my hands were wet and I expended several matches before I managed to get a light. Although I could have sworn I was standing straight up, I realised that I was wrong. Instead of pressing my back against the snow to leave a clear space in front, as I had imagined, I was actually leaning that way. Changing my direction as indicated, I began to burrow again, and soon the snow became much looser and began to fall in of its own accord. I had to work fast to get something to stand on and raise me up. Then a whole lot of snow came down and I had a momentary glimpse of bright sunlight. Once again I was buried under a cascade of loose snow, but the worst was over.

When I pushed my head above the snow, the picture I had formed of what I should see was the very opposite of the one which met my eyes. And until I sorted it out I had the odd feeling that I had come up in a strange place.

The twenty feet drop over which I had jumped when descending the slope was now filled up with snow. I had been buried some fifteen feet down as far as I could estimate. Not far, but a depth at which a man can lose his life unless he can decide quickly which is the way out. For some time after that I had nightmares in which I was being buried in snow, and I decided that skiing was not as attractive as I had once imagined.

Dutch Green managed to winter in the wilds because he had the foresight to store provisions when few would be available. But how the wild creatures survived was something of a problem. The bears, of course, hibernated, living on their fat, and using it only slowly for they were in a state of coma.

The majority of the animals, however, did not hibernate. There was a dearth of nourishing food; conditions were severe due to the biting cold and the deep snow, and the animals needed extra energy in order to move about at all. How they kept alive seemed to me nothing short of miraculous, and having little idea as to how they did it, I read books on the subject.

These told me that all the animals stored fat to some extent during the summer and drew on it in the winter. That was obvious as the animals were fat in the fall and thin in spring. But this was only a fraction of the explanation. The fat might last an active animal six weeks, but hardly any more than that, and winter lasted six months.

This was certainly true of the moose, but concerning this creature the books simply gave him his technical name of *Alces Machlis Americana,* explained that it was a type of elk which lived on young shoots of various plants and leaves, and that it yarded up in winter. But I needed to know more than that, for leaves and young

shoots are not to be found in the Rockies after the first
hard frost, and the many moose tracks I had seen during
the winter in my district belied the yarding up theory.
They did yard up, it is true, but my investigations led me
to believe that they did so only sporadically, during the
blizzards and the severely cold periods which usually
followed them. But they soon deserted the yards, fending
for themselves individually, and managing to live somehow in their usual stamping grounds.

Having time to spare, I decided to make an effort to
see how the animals succeeded in surviving the winter.
Annie, the Wind Lake moose, provided me with the
information I needed as far as her kind was concerned.
There were several moose in the district, but only her
tracks appeared in my vicinity. During severe spells,
when all tracks were hidden beneath fresh snow, she
disappeared for as many as seven or eight days, and I
saw neither her nor her tracks.

Where she went I don't know, but it seems that the
moose over a large area gathered together in what the
zoologists call a yard, where they kept the snow around
them trampled down. I tried on one occasion to follow
Annie to her yard, but the going proved too tough for

me to find out where it was. She would break out a known
trail back to her own domain, and then branch off to
break a new trail through six to eight feet of snow.

On these side trails every spruce tip, every dormant
bud and spur of willow and alder was nibbled off as high
as she could reach. It was the same with the dry moss and
lichen that grew on the north side of the trees. Even some
of the bark was stripped and eaten. As soon as one of
these trails had been cleared of all that she could reach,
she started another one, battling through deep snow for
a considerable distance. Yet the diet, obtained by such
an expenditure of energy, was anything but nourishing.
Nor was the grass she sometimes ate from the ground
where my horses pastured in summer. To reach this she
had to dig through the snow with nose and hoofs, and
the grass she obtained was itself anaemic and had but
the barest food value.

But in eating the grass Annie was unconsciously
making nonsense of the opinions of the experts who had
written my books. For, according to them, a moose cannot
eat grass, its legs being too long for its mouth to reach
the ground. Annie, however, was not that kind of a moose.
But she was the kind who, like all her kind, got through
six savage winter months on what seemed to be a starva-
tion diet.

The smaller members of the deer family ate the same
things, but they lacked the long reach of the moose. They
certainly yarded up, however, but not until they were
compelled to do so. I encountered their tracks when there
were two feet of snow, but none were to be found when
it became too deep for them to get around in comfort.

The " yards " are formed by a number of deer gathering
together and keeping an area trampled flat. Within that
area they eat everything within reach that is edible. They
gradually enlarge the area, so that a yard ultimately
covers a large space. When seen in summer there can be
no mistaking it. It is bare of every scrap of lichen and
moss; all the undergrowth is cleared, and all the branches
within reach are stripped, the bark included. The

existence of the deer in the bleak, hostile winter months must be very precarious. Not only is food exceedingly scarce, but during a blizzard they must keep on the move practically the whole time in order to keep a small space open.

It would seem that a cougar or wolf finding a yard would simply have to wait around, helping himself to the deer at his leisure. Had this been the case all the deer would have perished long since. They are better able to protect themselves than is generally imagined. Proof of this was provided by a yard on which were found the bones of two deer and a cougar. Deer will fight when cornered, and in the breeding season it is wise not to interfere with them, for they can be quite dangerous. The bones of the cougar and the deer told their own stories. The cougar had raided the yard and killed a couple of victims, but that was as far as he was allowed to go. Being too long on the job of getting away with his prey all the deer in the yard had attacked him at once and the cougar had been given no chance.

Although the deer had a tough existence in winter, they seemed to fare better than the mountain sheep and goats. The snow was much too deep for them to come down into the valleys, but the weather was too savage for them to remain on their summer heights. To all intents and purposes they might have grown wings and migrated for the winter.

In fact, they remained on the exposed slopes or in their vicinity, which were kept clear by the wind. I searched those slopes dozens of times for sight of a sheep or goat, but every bush and rock had its drift of snow on the down wind side, and these countless patches of white on the hillside made the animals virtually invisible. One day, however, thinking that one of these patches moved, I made a laborious climb to confirm the fact that I had actually seen a sheep. Even when I was only five hundred yards away it was difficult to identify the sheep, but there they were. There were goats, too, and I had solved the problem of how they survived the winter.

Even so it was incredible that they managed to keep themselves alive. Their food was limited to dead grass, twigs from bushes, lichen and anything else they could pass into their stomachs, no matter how indigestible and lacking in nourishment it might seem. And on such a thin intake they were bound to live on the most exposed slopes, where the wind cleared the snow for them, but blew bitingly and cuttingly as it did so. Probably during the blizzards they retired to more sheltered quarters, but they were tough indeed to winter on such fare and under such severe conditions.

There were many kinds of smaller animals which had to face up to the chill wilderness. As far as food was concerned perhaps the snowshoe rabbit had the easiest time. He hopped freely on the surface of the snow, and the drifts often rose to such a height that they gave him access to the tender bark and buds well up in the trees. But the snowshoe rabbit figured prominently on the menus of many of the flesh eaters both large and small. They might drop on him out of the sky, or come up at him from below. Or, as in the case of the fox and wolf, they might rush on him over the top as soon as the snow had settled sufficiently to prevent them sinking too deeply to rob them of their speed. The life of the snowshoe rabbit, in fact, was most uncertain and must have been anything but restful.

Although there were a number of marten in the district, I rarely came upon their tracks in the winter. The marten is a fierce little animal very much like a large weasel, and in summer he is to be seen running up and down trees with an amazing agility. His movements are so smooth and graceful that he appears to glide like a shadow. He preys on rabbits, squirrels, young birds and other small creatures.

The absence of marten tracks in winter raised the question as to how he secured his food and where he was spending his time. One day, happening on some marten tracks, I examined them. But they seemed merely to circumvent a tree two or three times and that was all, yet the tree revealed no sign of the marten. Then I saw more tracks near another tree, and closer investigation brought to my notice the remains of a rabbit. The marten had made several trips from the tree to the rabbit and this made it obvious where he had gone.

When the snow is deep the swaying of a tree in the wind causes a space to form by the snow being pressed away from the trunk. This may be helped by the slightly higher temperature of the trunk conducting warmth from the ground, or down on those days when the temperature rises. The space formed is not very noticeable as the top of the gap is nearly always covered by loose snow. But here it was quite plain that the marten had gone down the tree much as he did in summer, and I discovered that nearly every tree for some distance revealed a few tracks, plus the holes in the snow beside the trunks. Evidently I was in the middle of a small colony of marten, and it was obvious that they used the trees in winter as much as in summer, by burrowing along the ground beneath the snow, moving from tree to tree.

I now understood the ridges of snow I had seen sometimes in the spring. These ridges were sprawled all over the place when all the other snow had gone, lasting about a day or so longer than the rest of the snow. Thus to see them it was necessary to be in the right place at the right time. They were caused by marten and other small creatures pushing their way beneath the snow and so packing it just that slight amount more tightly than the rest.

A considerable amount of life, it was clear, went on beneath the snow, for where it was deep it was comparatively warm; so much so that in places the ground did not freeze at all or only very slightly. It was highly probable that squirrels and chipmunks, thought to hibernate throughout the winter, sometimes ventured out to augment their winter food reserves with seeds and dried berries hidden beneath the snow.

My observations also led me to wonder whether the squirrels and chipmunks fell victim to the marten, mink

and ermine while making these forays, thus providing
these creatures with supplies of food. Few naturalists
have made a study of these possibilities, for conditions in
the mountains and forests in winter are so severe that
observation is exceedingly difficult. Yet it is only in these
places that the snow is deep enough for life to continue
largely undetected, and it may well be that much more
is going on in the depths of winter than the experts have
so far imagined.

Throughout the winter I kept a lookout for traces of
mink. Not being a trapper, however, I did not know just
where to look. This little creature which provides the
pelts so beloved of film stars, is capable of producing an
odour that is almost as repellent as that of the skunk.
Much like the marten in appearance, he is aquatic rather
than an animal of the trees. At least, in summer he carries
out his hunting in the water. But I could not imagine
mink catching fish in winter when there are several feet
of ice on the lakes and rivers, and when the shallower
reaches of the creeks are quite solid. Once out of the
water, the wet fish would freeze and so, I thought, would
the wet mink.

Yet this apparently reasonable assumption proved to
be false, and I came upon evidence that the mink is able
to continue his fishing even in places where the ice was
at its thickest. Travelling along the glare ice of the lake
one cold, sunny morning, I saw the only mink I happened
upon all winter. He came out from a snow bank beside
the lake, scampered over the ice for a short distance, then
he caught sight of me. Promptly he doubled back again.

Generally the wind kept the lake swept clear of snow,
but the surrounds were hidden beneath great drifts,
sometimes as much as twenty feet high. The mink had
disappeared beneath one of these drifts, and I went over
to investigate. Finding the barely visible hole into which
the mink had vanished was far from easy. Having located
it, I burrowed in for several feet, reaching the edge of
the lake. There the little tunnel widened out and was
obviously well used. Its sides were coated with ice, and

where it started there was, between the bank of the lake
and the ice, a space about three inches wide. In this
space, some twelve inches down, there was water.

At this point the bank was so steep as to be almost
vertical, and with a stick I found that I could reach down
into the water right to the bottom of the ice. Either the
mass of snow allowed the higher temperature of the earth
or rock to melt the ice just those few inches, or there was
a little spring down below. Maybe both factors explained
the presence of the water. In any case, there was a way
for the mink to reach the lake beneath the ice, in spite
of the fact that the ice maintained its thickness of several
feet right to the edge of the lake with the exception of
that narrow crack.

This allowed the mink to get at the plentiful supply of
fish in the lake and take it to a place deep under the snow
or perhaps to its summer den in the bank. There the
mink would shake the water from its coat before it froze
and eat the fish in comfort. This subterranean navigation
would of necessity be most exact, as the mink would have
to find its way out again in almost pitch darkness far
beneath the ice.

In summer I have often seen mink swimming half
submerged, very like a small otter, then diving and staying submerged for an incredible length of time before
returning to the surface. In winter, however, their under-
ice hunting seemed to be a very risky business.

My investigations had to be discontinued as a fall of
snow buried me owing to the fact that I had disturbed
the base of the drift. But the few fish scales I discovered
were proof that the mink did indeed go fishing even
under the most unlikely conditions.

Winter seems to create no difficulties for the fish. They
stay near the bottom of their haunts in a state of lethargy,
their tails and fins moving just sufficiently to preserve
their balance, the gills slowly opening and closing. In
creeks they move into the deeper pools to avoid being
frozen in, but even when they become iced up it seems
to have no effect on them.

When wintering on the ranch I used to cut a quantity
of ice from a deep pool in the creek and store it in saw-
dust for the summer. I always found a large shoal of fish
in this pool beneath the ice in a state of partially suspended animation. I have also found them frozen in the
ice, and when allowed to thaw out slowly and naturally
they have seemed none the worse for their chill imprison-
ment. When the thaw came I have examined the pool
and never once have I found dead fish. But as frogs, toads
and other cold blooded creatures must freeze up and
recover, it is not surprising that fish should do the same.

The birds face up to winter according to their nature
and habits. The great white owl, which has a wing span
of from four to five feet, is as white as the snow itself. He
sails down the aisles of the forest at night at considerable
speed, but so quietly that there is not even a whisper of
disturbed air as he passes. To encounter him after dark
is an eerie experience, for he is as much like a ghost as
any creature I have seen. His winter food is the rabbit,
and his speed, silent approach and keen eyesight ensure
that few prospective victims escape him.

At the other extreme there is the chickadee, a most
intriguing bird. Slight and similar to a tit, with silvery
grey body and black cap, he is a cheerful creature, dart-
ing about in search of food from daylight to dark. This
bird certainly knows where the flies go to in winter time.
Hanging upside down, he peers into every crack and
cranny, poking about the rough bark of old trees and
devouring, at the rate of several a minute, the dehydrated
insects which hide there. He is a cheerful little creature.
No matter how cold it is his cheerful chick-a-dee-dee-dee
is not silenced. With his happy cry he challenges the
fiercest blizzard, flying from the sheltered side of one tree
to another. His life is a busy one, for he must have food
every minute of the day when they are at their shortest
and coldest, otherwise he would not survive the long and
bitter nights.

The balance between life and death is very finely
drawn for the chickadee. Their natural enemies are many,

and their tiny, rapidly beating hearts must keep up an extremely rapid circulation, or else their slender, pin-like legs would freeze solid in seconds. Thus, although the chickadee is small, an adequate supply of fuel is even more essential to it than to a creature which is larger and which can do without food for a time without suffering any ill effects. Let the chickadee be anything but in the best condition when temperatures are from fifty to sixty degrees below zero, and it cannot survive for more than a few minutes. A chickadee which I noticed was not quite its fleet, gay self, was alive one minute and a tiny block of ice some sixty seconds later.

The extreme opposite of the busy little chickadee is, of course, the bear. Throughout the chill months of winter it is in a sleep that is almost a coma, needing nothing more in the way of food than the fat stored in its own body. Yet where the bears indulge their protracted annual sleep is something of a mystery. Never once did I succeed in finding the hideout of a bear. On one occasion I followed a trail in the snow which, I think, would have led me to where a bear was hibernating. But the way was too far and too difficult for me to continue to the end of the journey.

Bears, however, present several very intriguing problems. It is astonishing that such a large creature can store enough in the way of nutritional reserves to last it for five or six months. But it seems that the female bear does much more than that. For it is required to feed one and even two youngsters on occasion, and to feed them so well that from tiny naked things not much larger than a baby rabbit, they develop by the spring into fat balls of fluff the size of small dogs. And the reserves of the female bear have to serve for her offspring as well as for herself.

Bears, it would seem, judging by their size and strength, would feed in a gargantuan fashion, eating huge meals very frequently. They do have such a feed occasionally, and particularly at spawning time when the higher reaches of the creeks are swarming with fish. Yet such enormous repasts are very much the exception. Most

of the time bears feed on roots and berries, and occasionally on a small animal. That such fare should even keep
them going is amazing. But it does much more than that,
for it makes them remarkably fat. Although they have
enormous appetites, as is evident by what they eat when
the opportunity occurs, generally their diet seems more
suitable to a creature the size of a spruce partridge than
to a full grown bear.

They eat in a most leisurely manner as I was made to
realise when watching them feed on blueberries. They
displayed no hurry, as any creature might who had to
put away large reserves for the winter. Instead, they sat
up and licked their paws from time to time and looked
round at the scenery as though admiring its beauty. It
seemed to me a miracle that they were ever ready to face
the five or six months of fasting, but it was a miracle that
undoubtedly occurred.

My winters in Sikanaska convinced me that there was
far more activity in the wild than we have so far sus-
pected. The animals, of course, were clothed to withstand
even the most severe conditions. A man who is
equipped to keep out the frost can find the winter by no
means unpleasant. There is danger in such a savage cold,
but the atmosphere is dry. It is so dry, in fact, that I have
slipped out of my cabin in stockinged feet, the flour-like
snow shaking off without leaving even a trace of damp-
ness. A steel implement may be left out all winter and it
will betray no signs of rust. The intense cold lingers
throughout the winter, but apart from the occasional
gentle snowstorm, or the more infrequent blizzard, there
is brilliant sunshine which, though lacking warmth, is
cheerful. The skies are cloud free most of the time, and
at night, because of the remarkable clarity of the air, the
stars shine with an unimpaired brilliance.

VI: BUSH PILOT

ON THE RARE occasions when I wintered in the mountains the decision was made in good time, allowing me opportunity to transport my provisions before the first snows fell. Once, however, the decision to take measurements of the water flow in the creeks and river was taken very belatedly.

The passes were much too dangerous for horses, and it was decided to fly me in, which meant that the plane would have to land on the lake. The air above the mountains being exceedingly turbulent, planes crossed them only at great heights or else over known routes where the mountains are comparatively low.

In the ordinary way no landing would have been attempted, but the readings were regarded as necessary and it was decided that the trip must be made. If I remember rightly, the plane engaged for the job was a Stinson Detroiter, and the first sight of it surprised me. It was by no means new, and was obviously incapable of attaining the height deemed necessary for safe flying in mountain areas. The pilot, Vic Hamilton, did much to restore my confidence, for he was a cool individual, not likely to be disturbed by anything short of an earthquake.

We got away all right and managed to climb to some nine thousand feet above take off level, or some twelve thousand feet above sea level. We crossed the first two ridges, which were not too high, flying between the loftier peaks, where we encountered little wind and no turbulence of such a nature that it caused us anxiety.

Hamilton, however, was unwilling to risk being caught and tossed about by air currents and we dropped down right into the valley in the vicinity of Sikanaska. From here we followed the valley at a height of no more than two hundred feet, and the terrain was well-known to me, for I had travelled it often on horseback. The scenery rushed by, and a journey that normally took me hours to complete was covered in a matter of minutes. Reaching the large amphitheatre which I called the crossroads, I motioned that it was here that we had to turn right.

" Are you sure this is it?" Vic shouted.

I nodded, and down we went to land on the ice without so much as a bump. We taxied swiftly to the head of the lake and came to a halt. The wind had cleared the snow from the lake for us, but it had not been so obliging on land. We had to break a trail through to the cabin, and by the time all my gear had been transported Hamilton had time only for a quick meal.

" I've no wish to be benighted or stormbound," he said. " But I'm expecting an easy journey back when the plane has only me to carry."

I went down to the lake to see him off, and he walked round the plane and gave a few turns to a nut. Upon closer inspection I saw that this was nothing more than a square-headed iron bolt which can be bought in any hardware store and actually was part of an elevator hinge. I was glad I hadn't noticed this before, for it suggested that the plane was by no means certain to remain in one piece, and the knowledge would have made my trip in an anxious business.

Vic swung the propeller a few turns and then switched on. Another turn and the engine should have started up, but it failed to do so. Vic swung the propeller again; then I swung it. In fact, we swung it so long and with such vigour that we were nearly exhausted.

"I'll get this plane into the air," Vic threatened, "if it's the last thing I do."

In his determination to achieve action, he warmed up the cylinders with a blow lamp, while I stood by with a fire extinguisher in case of fire. There was no fire, but there was no response from the engine, either, in spite of more prop swinging. Examination revealed that the ignition was all right, but that gas was not getting through properly. The light was failing, and it was too risky repairing the gas line and taking off that day.

"Guess I'll have to stay over till morning," Vic said, not in the least perturbed. "But I must get away early, before they start looking for us. You go and get some grub ready and I'll see if I can find what's holding up the gas."

The meal was ready when he arrived, his hands half frozen as he carried a carburettor and an assortment of pipes. Having eaten, he thawed the filter and pipes and cleaned out of them a large amount of sludge.

"That should be O.K.," he said. "It was letting her get cold that did it. Up north in the summer the filter gets filled up with mosquitoes and all sorts of muck, especially when you use a funnel with a busted gauze for gassing up."

Mr Hamilton's nonchalant attitude towards his plane surprised me, but it was not my place to tell this bush pilot that it would be a wise precaution to check up on his plane before trouble occurred.

Nevertheless, Vic Hamilton belonged to a body of men who have won international fame because of their courage and high sense of duty. It was the bush pilots Roy Brown and Wop May who carried some serum in an ancient open cockpit plane in the dead of winter to Aklavik. They refuelled at dumps on the Mackenzie River, landing on treacherous, bumpy ice. They dug the drums of gas out of the deep snow, and heated a couple of bricks to keep the serum from freezing.

This was but one of the mercy flights undertaken by these bush pilots, and which were often made at their own expense. They seemed to bear charmed lives, for they had a very happy-go-lucky attitude towards the maintenance of their planes, much of which they had to undertake themselves on the job, yet very few of them came to grief.

All had hair raising experiences, Vic Hamilton among them, and as I had done a bit of flying in the First World War, he opened up and told me a story he had told to very few others. I happened to remember reading an account of a pilot called Hamilton who had been lost in the bush, and I asked Vic if he was the same person.

" I guess I was," he said. "I'd been given the job of collecting a couple of trappers from Fort Norman, who were to be taken west. We were to look for virgin trapping country, which is plentiful thereabouts, and when they saw the sort of country they were looking for, I was to land 'em on the nearest lake. I was then to return to Fort Norman, collect the rest of their stuff and get it to them.

" That region is real wild. Most of the main lakes and rivers have been mapped, it's true, but they haven't all been marked in the right places. Besides, there's so many creeks and lakes that haven't been mapped at all that it's all too easy to get mixed up.

" The trappers were paying me five hundred dollars for the job, so I didn't mind taking a little trouble for them, and we had as much stuff aboard as I could carry. But we managed to get safely over the range, and they told me the heavily timbered country beyond was just to their liking. Then we spotted a lake that promised to be just the thing we needed for landing. It was away from any waterways that were of any size and it seemed certain that it was in country where there had never been any trapping. It was a very isolated spot about midway between Fort Norman and Dawson City. I put down, unloaded, and made a rough map that was good enough for me to find the place again. But just to make sure

ST7*

there would be no mistake, I told 'em to make smoke when they heard me coming back the next day.

"The precaution proved unnecessary. I got the rest of their stuff in without any difficulty, and left them, having arranged to get them out the following spring with their pelts, either before the ice went, or on floats just after it had gone.

"The other bush pilots were at Slave Lake on a job hauling some stuff up to the Bear, and I intended to join them. I set a course that would bring me to the Mackenzie River just below Simpson, where I meant to refuel and go on to Slave Lake.

"I'd covered around fifty miles when my engine went dead. I was some three thousand feet up, and the only place I could see to set her down was a lake which was about half the size I needed to make a comfortable landing. A dead stick landing's difficult enough even when there's plenty of room. Dead scared of undershooting, I came in a bit high. Not enough for any S turns or the like, but just too high. I sideslipped all I could, but still ran up the far bank and brought up with the nose between two trees. One blade was broken off the prop and the other was bent.

"I climbed out and surveyed the damage. Apart from the prop I'd done nothing worse than hole one of the floats. I knew someone would be looking for me in a day or two, but I knew if they tried to get down to me in such a place there was a risk that we'd both be stuck. It was my hope that I could get them to drop me a new prop, and then, when I'd cut some trees at one end of the lake and made the plane as light as I could by dumping everything I didn't need, get her out.

"We all carried a light camping outfit, some grub and a .22 rifle, so I made myself at home and got ready to wait. I discovered that I'd had to come down because some worn ignition leads had shorted through the frame, cutting out both mags. at once. I propped up the float, repaired it and got the old crate afloat again.

"I built a fire ready to light up, and I'd green alder

boughs on hand to make a smoke, and I was all ready to
be rescued. Some days later, hearing a plane, I got my
smudge going, but the wind carried it into the trees and
it didn't rise far. If seen at all it would have looked like
a patch of haze, and that's all. The plane passed, and a
couple of days later I saw an Air Force plane a few miles
away. I did everything I knew to draw his attention, but
it was no good. He was obviously looking for me, and he
returned on his search down the other side of the lake,
but without seeing me. That was the last plane I saw on
the lookout for me, although, as I learnt later, a dozen
were hunting for me for the best part of a week. Not
having the least idea where I was, they might have been
looking for a grain of salt in a heap of snow, for in such
country there's no lack of area in which to look.

" It was then that I remembered that I'd not told a soul
where I was likely to be. And I remembered something
else. No one but me knew where the trappers were, and
it would be just as difficult finding them in the spring as
it was finding me right then.

" I had to decide what to do. At most I'd only two
months in which to travel before winter set in. I could
start hiking towards the Mackenzie River, but what with
virgin forest, the Mackenzie Range and muskeg, I might

be a couple of months before I struck the river. No one would be using it so late in the year, and I might still be a long way from Fort Norman. I'd be delayed by having to hunt my grub as I went, for the only food I had was a small supply of dry stuff.

"The plan seemed to me to be too risky to adopt. To be caught unprepared by the winter might well mean that I wouldn't survive. Nor could I go the other way. I didn't know the country to the West, and I might follow a big creek thinking it would lead to the Yukon River, and thus find myself bushed, again with winter on my neck.

"I decided the wisest course was to stay where I was, build a dugout and get together as much grub as I could. There were lots of fish in the lake and quite a lot of game around. Providing I survived the winter I could start out for the Mackenzie in the spring.

"I was no great shakes as a woodsman, but I was handy with tools, and it was that which gave me my idea. Could I make a prop? It was just possible that I could adapt what I had to the job. The propeller would be far from the machine-made article, but if it served to fly me out of the place where I was caught, then it would do all that was necessary. If not, then the end for me would be quicker than freezing or starving to death, which was likely to be my fate if I had to winter in the wilds.

"I got to work right away. Choosing a dead spruce that was seasoned but sound, I began to shape it. It was hard work, and what with the time lost in hunting grub and not having all the tools I needed, it took me the best part of three weeks to finish the job. But I was proud of it when it was completed. In outward appearance it was exactly like the old one, for I'd been mighty particular about the measurements. My cutting tools were only a small axe and a knife, and I'd had to take off the rough edges with sandstone. I had it balanced to a nicety, spending a lot of time smoothing a bit off here and there and making as sure of it as I could.

"I had made a block of wood to fill the centre hole and I'd made an axle from the tommy bar of a box spanner. I swung the prop until it had no heavy spots and would stop wherever it slowed down. Heated red hot that tommy bar was the right size for the bolt holes, too. I had long since sealed up all vents so that no gas would evaporate, and I could see no reason why I should not be all right providing I could get out of the lake.

" I cut down some trees at the end the prevailing wind came from, and the tops off some trees farther back, giving myself a reasonable chance of clearing them, as long as I managed to get my floats unstuck in time. All I needed now was a wind.

" I had everything in readiness for it. I'd unloaded everything I could, even all my tools. I'd started up the motor and revved her up, and I was glad to note that there was little more than the normal vibration. Then the wind blew up from the right direction. I towed the plane to the far end of the lake, the wind giving me plenty of help, and tied the tail skid to a tree with a piece of cord. I was hoping to get up full revs before the cord broke and thus have a good send off without wasting any space.

" I warmed up, and the old crate was pulling at the cord when I gave her the gun. The cord snapped and the machine fairly leapt forward. Then there was a horrible crash, and a vibration that threatened to take the motor right out of the frame, so I cut. And there I was with half a prop, one blade having snapped near the hub. I was feeling pretty despondent, as you can guess, but I'd been lucky. Had the propeller broken a few seconds later I'd have crashed into the bank at the far side of the lake. As it was the initial impetus had almost carried me there.

" I jumped out into shallow water, made the plane fast near my camp and examined the other blade of the prop. It was quite sound. I guess my timber had been that much too seasoned and was just a shade brittle. Anyway, all I got out of my three weeks' work was a bit of fuel for my fire.

" I was in a tight corner now. I'd spent a lot of time that should have been devoted to catching and smoking fish, and getting game, and making other preparations for the winter. The first snows could not be more than four weeks away and might well be much less.

"I was ruminating darkly over my position when a voice behind me said, 'How!'

"I nearly left my boots. The speaker was an Indian, a Yellow Knife, the only kind up that way, and even they are very few in numbers. Except for the Esquimos they are the only human beings between where I was and the North Pole. They still live much as they used to do before the white man set foot in Canada, but they visit one of the posts about once a year for trade. The chances of finding Yellow Knife Indians in my vicinity were a million to one, but it had come off. Whatever happened, I wasn't going to starve to death in a bitter winter.

"'Where did you spring from?' I asked.

"He had only the scraps of English he had picked up on his visits to the trading posts, but he was quick on the uptake.

"'Me winter camp that way,' he said, waving towards the west. 'Me hunt and hear big noise, and come look.' He pointed at the plane. 'Him bust plenty.'

"I asked him what my chances were of getting out before winter, and he shook his head.

"'Too far. No good. Indian stay by teepee. You stay teepee, too.'

"So far so good. I could stay with the Indians until spring, and maybe learn something about living near the Arctic in winter. I told him my name, but he had not been to any of the trading posts recently and could not have heard that I was missing. As for his name, I failed to get it, as it was one of those long ones which mean a lot to Indians, but which mean nothing to us. We compromised with Kawa, which was a part of his name, and the one by which he was known at the posts.

"I showed him the broken propeller, explained how I had made one and how it had broken. He examined the old prop carefully.

"'Ugh!' he grunted. 'Him make plenty little woods all stickum same one piece.'

" That, of course, was his way of saying laminated, and though he said no more, as I discovered later on, he gave the matter a great deal of thought.

" As I was short of food, Kawa insisted that I should join his camp. This consisted of a couple of families, and how they found their way around the country was a mystery to me. He took me to the camp by what must have been to him a known path, though he might well have been over it only once. For we ran into no cul-de-sac of windfalls and we didn't have to turn back once. Yet there was no sign of a trail as far as I could see. It was the same when they travelled to the trading posts. Anyone else would have been continually retracing their steps to find a way around something or other, but not those Yellow Knife Indians. Yet their trails were so little used that they never in any way resembled a beaten track.

" Horses could not be used up there, for there was not enough food for them and there were plenty of places where horses could not be taken. They packed their huskies in the summer, and those dogs carried loads which amazed me. The huskies pulled their toboggans in winter, and what couldn't be carried this way the Indians packed on their backs.

" These families were all set for a winter's trapping and had a sheltered camp near a creek. After the best meal I'd had since coming down on the lake, Kawa took me to a tree from which hung some long strips of timber, drying out. I never found out how they managed to make them that way, but I was certainly amazed by them. They were about eight feet long and six inches wide, by half an inch thick, and were as smooth and even as if cut in a sawmill and finished off on a planing machine. They were used for their toboggans, which were more useful to them than sleds as the snow over which they travelled was often soft and unbroken. Kawa indicated the pieces of wood and said:

" 'Piece wood all same thing that bust.' Then, going to a balsam, he came back with some gum and with a trium-

phant grin said, ' Stickum,' as if making a new prop was
as good as done.

" It was an idea worth trying, and I arranged with
Kawa to pack the wood to the lake and keep me supplied
with food. That way I could devote all my time to making
another propeller. In exchange I promised him my rifle
and all the other things I should be leaving behind, and
he was delighted.

" He and half the members of his numerous family
carried the pieces of wood and food to the lake, and I got
to work on the new prop. I had a can of marine glue for
fixing floats and used it, figuring it might be stronger than
balsam gum. I laid the strips of timber out in a double
ended fan roughly the shape of the prop, glued them well
and weighted them down with rocks to set. The only snag
was that they did not come wide enough at the hub to
take all the bolts. But I could get four of them in and
filled up with a solid block of wood so that it would
tighten up evenly. I made the holes as before, then
thought I might further strengthen it by binding it. I
asked Kawa to bring me some more balsam gum and a
pot in which to melt it. Then I cut my groundsheet into
strips, dipped this in the hot gum and bound the prop
tightly with it. When it was set it was like a solid case,
but it was slightly out of balance. By taking a bit off the
tip of the heavy end, however, I achieved a perfect
balance once more.

" Ready once more, I started up the motor, this time
with the floats against the bank. Then revving to full
throttle, I cut the engine suddenly. I did this several
times, and the prop held.

" I explained to Kawa that I would like him to help me
with the take off and supply me with a good length of
rope or rawhide. All the Indians turned up to see the
performance, making a temporary camp at the lake side.
They helped by removing more trees and topping off
others. While waiting for the wind I rehearsed with Kawa
what he was to do at the take off, and he quickly understood what I wanted him to do. He was a good feller,

and I believe he would have done everything for me had there been nothing in it for him. As it was I told him to be sure and go to Fort Norman the following summer, as there would be a credit awaiting him there.

"When the wind did blow in from the right direction it was not as strong as I really needed it to be, but I dare wait no longer. We drifted down the lake with Kawa helping to fend off and guide. The tail skid was fastened to a tree with rawhide and Kawa stood in the water near the tail ready with his knife.

"I warmed up the engine, then opened to full throttle. The rawhide fairly stretched, and the prop still held. I raised my hand, the straining plane was released and she leapt forward. I've never got off so quickly in my life, but in spite of that the floats brushed through some of the taller trees. But the propeller fouled nothing, and I was clear. I levelled off, circled and waved to the Indians. Then I was away.

"I reached Fort Norman without mishap, and there was quite a sensation when a supposedly dead man turned up complete with his plane. I'd been given up, the general opinion being that I'd crashed and been killed.

"I'd given Kawa a rough map of where the trappers were, just in case I didn't make the Fort, but he never had need to use it. I went in for those trappers at the time they were expecting me, and got them out without a hitch. As for Kawa, he turned up at the Post all right the following summer and collected the fifty dollars I'd left for him. But I didn't happen to be around at the time, and I've never seen him since."

That was Vic Hamilton's story, and it was true all right. In fact, the propeller he made has been on show at various places since the day he landed at Fort Norman after being missing for two months and given up for dead.

VII : ONE EAR

ALTHOUGH IT SOMETIMES happened that the Forestry Superintendent had a job for me in winter, I more often spent my winters on the ranch attending to various chores. Sometimes winter was long delayed, no snow falling until Christmas or even later, although, of course, there would be snow on the mountains at the higher altitudes. The nights were cold, often down to zero, but the days were glorious, being warmed by brilliant sunshine. At such times the Canadian West has a climate rarely equalled anywhere in the world.

It was during such a long delayed onset of winter that I became interested in One Ear. One Ear was a rabbit and, as the name I gave him suggests, he was easy to recognise because he had lost an ear. He had been around for some years, and this in itself was remarkable. For the life of a rabbit in the bush is a thing of constant peril. From the day of its birth, death is rarely more than a yard or two behind it, a few feet in front of it, or hovers above it in the skies.

The rabbit seems born to a brief life of endless caution, for its enemies are legion. It figures prominently as a savoury dish for humans, who trap and shoot it. And in the bush it must always be on the alert for the fox, the marten, the ermine and the coyote, as well as ready to flee from other animals which move swiftly, wait cunningly and overtake without warning. Even this host of enemies does not exhaust the list. For the owl and the hawk drop out of the sky swiftly and with but little sound, and their talons frequently seize the unprotected rabbit.

In addition, the rabbit must come to terms with the elements, and these are often hostile.

The rabbit has survived only because of his frequent breeding, which means that an immense wastage is constantly replaced. In addition, he is protected by his colouring which changes to suit his condition, and also because he is not quite as stupid as some people imagine.

The life of a rabbit in the bush being generally so very short, the fact that One Ear survived so very long was intriguing. There must, I decided, be something rather special about him. Even a rabbit profits by experience providing it lives long enough, and the fact that it has remained alive one year strengthens its chances of living throughout its second year. And One Ear had been in evidence for no less than five years, which made him a veteran amongst rabbits. In that time he had evidently learnt enough tricks to keep him alive until age reduced his speed and dimmed his senses. Then he would become the victim of one of the many enemies he had so far eluded. But what his age would be then I had no idea.

In appearance the snowshoe rabbit is much like his English cousins, but he has slightly longer and broader hind legs. When the toes are spread out they leave a track resembling a snowshoe, and the spread enables them to stay on top when the snow is quite soft. Unlike their English cousins, they have their young at the rate of only two at a time.

I was walking through the bush one morning in search of my horses, and where in the summer there would not have been a single rabbit to be seen, there were several dotted about, and sitting as motionless as if they had been

carved in white stone. As is the case with many furred
and feathered creatures of the north, snowshoe rabbits
turn white in the winter and are as hard to detect in the
snow as they are in the camouflage with which they are
provided in the summer. In fact, they are perhaps even
better protected in winter than in summer, for then there
is no white flash of tail to betray their presence when
they run.

These rabbits, apparently sitting in such foolish
prominence, were behaving quite sensibly. But nature
had betrayed them. Here was the proper season to be
white, when they were protected by keeping still against
the snow. But the snow had failed to arrive.

It was then that I spotted One Ear, but I was allowed
to glimpse him for only a second. He moved smartly
behind a tree, and though I moved round in order to
have another look at him, he moved too, keeping the tree
between us. None of the other rabbits displayed this
intelligence. Although some of them were quite close,
they all remained perfectly still. Here was food for
thought. With the exception of One Ear, all the rabbits
were acting instinctively, and in a way which, under the
conditions usual at that time of year, would have given
them the maximum safety. For against the snow, their
security depended upon them being still, for the only
part of the rabbit likely to catch attention was the eye.

Why, then, was One Ear behaving so much more
intelligently than the rest? The answer could only be that
he had acquired by experience rather more intelligence
than had the other rabbits. His retreat from the human
being was, I felt sure, connected with some experience
with humans, probably when he lost his ear. Sportsmen
from town often came shooting at these sitting targets
and it was possible that a near miss had drilled his ear
when it would subsequently freeze and fall off; hence he
might have learnt that it was not so good to sit still when
men were around.

I tried reconstructing his story, for it is not difficult for
one accustomed to the woods to read in tracks even

without the benefit of snow the history of events which have culminated in death, or escape, or in sudden flight.

In One Ear's case it was possible to be sure of many things. It was certain, for instance, that he had been born in a hole scooped out beneath the protruding root of a large tree. The hole was well hidden and the entrance was too small to admit any animal larger than a rabbit. The tough old root prevented any predatory creature from breaking it up from above, for the rabbit shows great wisdom when selecting his home.

Like the rabbit born with him, One Ear was tiny, pink, naked and blind. But their hole was lined with moss and fur and was warm and cosy. And One Ear was provided with all the food he needed by his mother, and when he wasn't eating he was sleeping.

After a while One Ear was able to see; he was no longer naked and he managed a few steps towards the light that found its way through the entrance to the hole. But the growing brightness would cause him to retreat to the darker recesses of his home.

He soon learnt to recognise his mother by sight as well as by smell and touch, but he was not to have her long. His mother had made one of several possible mistakes, and the kind of error which spells death to the lesser creatures of the bush. Having a family she was not likely to go far from her burrow, but one day she ventured a mere few feet too far into the open. That, however, was more than enough for the great owl which had its home in a giant jack pine. The owl had been patiently waiting for just such opportunity, and it did not waste it when it came. It swooped down silently upon her. To save herself she should have doubled back beneath the bird so that it would overshoot its mark. But the owl was so close when she became aware of its approach that she panicked and ran. That was a fatal mistake. There was a shrill scream as the talons sank home and then there was silence.

Normally, having no one to fend for him, One Ear should have grown hungrier, colder and weaker until he

died, and that is almost certainly what happened to the
rabbit which had been born with him. But this is not
what happened to One Ear, for it was now that he first
provided evidence that he possessed that something
extra which was to ensure him a ripe old age.

Hungrier than he had ever been before, he ventured to
the entrance of the hole, and there grew a tuft of grass.
He might have tried sucking this at first, but when
nothing came of this he would tackle it with his teeth.
He found that he liked grass, and also that it satisfied his
hunger.

After a while he felt warmer and stronger. His coat was
quite thick, and as the days passed he ventured farther
and farther from home. Always, however, he was on the
alert to dash back to the safety of his burrow the instant
he caught any scent or sound with which he was not
familiar. No doubt, in those early stages, he fled many
times when there was no need to do so. But he was eating
other things besides grass, and finding life as full of
interest as it was of peril. Although he was quick, he
survived those first few weeks of independence only
because he had a large measure of luck.

Eventually he deserted the hole altogether. Instinctively
he was acquiring a mental map of all the trails he used,
memorising every jump. Many of his enemies were much
more fleet than he was, and his life depended upon his
knowing exactly where to go to find refuge, and where
to change direction without slowing as he did so. To take
the wrong turning might have brought him to a windfall
through which he did not know his way.

When he rested he crouched, keeping perfectly still
with the exception of the twitching of his sensitive nose,
which registered even the faintest scent, and the turning
of his long ears, which, even when he slept, caught every
sound. A sound which warned of danger brought him to
full wakefulness in a split second.

Hearing the scream of one of his own kind he would
cautiously investigate. Finding that the killer was a
weasel, he would identify the scent as one that was

particularly dangerous. The scents of all his enemies, large and small, would be registered in the same way, and experience was affording him ever greater protection, although he lived constantly in a state of nervous expectation.

He would be full grown when he first changed colour and though he would be unaware of the change, he would find life very trying when snow failed to come; he would be so much more prominent to the owl and the coyote to say nothing of humans, but on the other hand one of his arch enemies the weasel or ermine as it is called when white would be easier to detect.

It was probably another of these winters of belated snow in his early life that taught him to keep out of sight of man. It is only surmise that a shot robbed him of his ear, but it would be unlikely that a bird or beast had come so near without finishing him off. Anyway we know he had found it best not to rely on keeping still when man was around, and without asking whether or not his camouflage was serving its proper function of making him nearly invisible, he would still nip smartly behind a tree when man hove in sight. This one unusual action gives him a very much above average I.Q. in the rabbit world and there is reason to suppose he excelled in other ways.

One Ear continued to grow larger and heavier. He found he was able to put to flight any rabbit trespassing upon his preserves, and he proved successful in avoiding all his natural enemies. He had all the time been gaining experience in their ways, and this served as a protection of an exceptionally high order for one of his kind. Because of his experience he was less likely to panic, and he was able to anticipate the approach of his enemies and also what they were likely to do when they pursued him.

Although it had a ferocity out of all proportion to its size, to One Ear the ermine was an insignificant animal. It was the traditional enemy of rabbits, but he refused supinely to await his doom when this little creature made his appearance, but faced up to it instead. Who knows when he encountered this animal decisively for the first time? But with snow to help tell the story, it was easy to see what had happened in one such encounter.

On this occasion, sensing the ermine's approach, One Ear moved away as usual. But it was winter, and the ermine, perhaps hungrier than usual, was persistent and followed up. One Ear, who was trying to doze, was annoyed by two or three such interruptions, and when the ermine approached yet again, One Ear lost his temper.

There was a fair amount of snow and the ermine was hard to see, even though there was a moon, but as he came nearer the black speck that was the tip of his tail, twitching to and fro, became visible. One Ear, contrary to custom, made no move, and the ermine stopped a couple of yards away. This was the chance for which he had been waiting, and he was justified in thinking that his supper was as good as won. One Ear, however, lay back his solitary ear and presented as formidable an appearance as possible to his enemy, but the ermine was not deterred. He circled, leapt in the air, making spitting noises as he did so, thus pursuing the hypnotising process which always worked so well. But this was one of the rare occasions when the method failed. One Ear was not to be hypnotised.

The ermine moved this way and that and several times completely circled One Ear, but always the rabbit was facing him, instead of sitting stupidly and allowing the fierce little creature to get behind him. Every attempt the ermine made to get behind his prey failed, and thus he was prevented from springing on the rabbit's back and sinking his sharp fangs into the back of One Ear's neck. And the ermine, frustrated, lost his patience, and the ferocity for which he is famous came into play.

He launched himself like an arrow at the rabbit, but he failed to land as he had intended. For One Ear also sprang into the air and met the ermine with his back feet. Those back feet had immense power, as every naturalist knows, and when they struck the ermine they knocked him back some considerable distance.

Whirling up in a flurry of snow, the ermine tried again, only to suffer the same kind of reception. Now boiling with rage, the ermine hissed and spat, perhaps intending that his ferocity would serve to subdue the rabbit. But, if so, he discovered that he was grievously mistaken. For on launching himself at One Ear for the third time he was met by a backward kick that caught him full in the face. That took much of the life out of him and he lay writhing in the snow. This was a chance One Ear did not miss. He jumped high, landing with both hind feet and all his weight plumb on top of the ermine, driving him down into the snow. Had the ground been hard the ermine would have perished there and then, for One Ear jumped on him again and again until there was quite a deep hole, with the ermine at the bottom of it.

Even after the rabbit tired of his sport and left him the ermine was some time in recovering. And when he finally crawled away, injured and chastened, he took care that his direction was the opposite of that taken by One Ear.

Thus the rabbit managed to live on and wax fat. Once a lynx moved into the area. He was much more to be feared than the ermine, for he lay motionless and watchful on the branch of a tree, and dropped on his prey, seemingly out of the very sky. He almost brought an end

ST8*

to One Ear's unusually long life, and his presence added a
new terror to the days. Whenever One Ear caught the
faintest scent of the lynx, he raced to the far end of his
beat, and this happened many times, until at last the
lynx was shot by one of the ranchers.

Then came the winter in which my attention was
drawn to this remarkable rabbit. Never before had the
snow been so long delayed, and its absence made life
more perilous than usual. Again and again he found himself eluding slashing fangs or grasping talons. Yet these
experiences did not interfere with his appetite. The
moment the danger was past, he would begin eating.
Mercifully, he was unable to anticipate the future, and
could not, therefore, people it with frightening possibilities.

Nevertheless, the owl kept making attempts upon his
life when he should have been invisible against the snow.
Because of this absence of snow, dogs, which he normally
avoided with ease, proved not quite so easy to slip.

He was sitting resting when he heard the coyote quest-
ing about for a scent. Instantly alert, One Ear waited.
The scent grew fresher, the coyote moved faster and
nearer, and the rabbit, aware that he was the coyote's
objective, made off with a few yards start. The coyote,
now hunting by sight and not by scent, his quarry's white
body showing up vividly, was overhauling his prey.

One Ear ran straight for a while, but his enemy gained
on him, and soon the hungry jaws were very close. Judging his speed with an exactness born of long experience,
the rabbit, reaching a run, turned off at right angles. He
leapt aside, doubled back, and in a flash he was on the
trail he had just left, streaking in the opposite direction.

The coyote overshot, skidded to a halt and turned. One
Ear's excellent judgment should have put an end to the
affair. He was quite some distance from the coyote and
was in no immediate hurry. But the coyote could still see
the white patch bobbing along in the distance and
promptly renewed the chase.

This sort of thing happened three or four times, and

One Ear adopted a different strategy. He ran fast along a zigzag trail with the coyote in close pursuit. A sharp turn and he dived through a dense tangle of windfalls and undergrowth where he knew his enemy could not follow. Here he squatted and saw the coyote rush around to the other side. Hopping back to where he had entered the tangle, the rabbit wandered along the back trail nibbling at some shoots.

The coyote, however, could still see the white form through the lattice of branches and twigs and tore round the windfall, in pursuit once more. One Ear left his spruce tips in a hurry and the chase was on again. He tore round almost the entire limits of his domain, the coyote still hanging on. But it was a winding way and One Ear maintained his lead.

Then he took an almost straight trail which led to the creek where he sometimes went for a drink in the summer. Now it was frozen and it had overflowed and frozen time and again until there was a broad stretch of ice from bank to bank. On a run that was almost straight the coyote was much the faster, but One Ear had not forgotten this fact. He was within a few yards of the creek when he slowed deliberately, allowing the coyote to come within a few inches of him. Then he dropped neatly down the foot or so of bank remaining above the ice and scuttled beneath it.

The coyote, with his quarry so near, was moving at full speed, making what should have been his final effort. In consequence he was going like the wind when he hit the ice. He made a desperate effort to twist and grab his prey as he passed over, failed to do so, and having no means of stopping, he slithered to the far bank where he came to a halt with a thud.

The rabbit did not see this, for the moment the coyote passed over him, he was away, heading for his stamping ground, intent on reaching its farthest limit. He ran with all the strength he could muster, for he was beginning to tire. The coyote, in trying to get up speed on the ice, fell over two or three times, and by the time he reached the bank One Ear was no longer in sight. The coyote was compelled to resort to scent again, and as he had climbed the bank a few yards from the point where he had left it, he picked up the trail of another rabbit which took him out of One Ear's area.

Then after a particularly harassing day, One Ear took advantage of a quiet spell to rest and settled for an uneasy nap. It became very dark, darker than it had been for a long time. The wind rose and howled and moaned in the trees, and the light he could see at the ranch house in the distance became dim and then faded out altogether.

Something wet and soft settled on One Ear's twitching nose. The flake was soon followed by another and yet another. It was snowing and it was snowing fast. One Ear was incapable perhaps of realising the importance of what was happening. But he was aware of change, and with it there came a greater sense of security. Now he could settle for the most undisturbed rest he had known for many weeks. Soon, buried in the snow, he could not be seen. He crouched, and only the twitching nose and the occasional movement of his one ear indicated that, even in the best of circumstances, he could never relax altogether.

Perhaps that wasn't quite One Ear's story, but I feel very sure that it was. For I witnessed him behaving on more than one occasion with an intelligence that was astonishing. And only such understanding and experience could explain how he had managed to survive so long. I still caught fleeting glimpses of him while I was in the area, and he must have been all of seven years. Which means that One Ear was a veritable Methuselah among rabbits.

VIII: THE WISDOM OF THE RED MAN

I OFTEN CAME upon Indians during my years in Sikanaska, and my admiration and affection for them grew the more I saw of them. Not that the Indians of North America are all Hiawathas which some romantics make them out to be. On the other hand, they are not the cruel, war loving savages of the Hollywood film.

In recent times the Indians of North America have become divided into groups. Some have achieved fame as poets and authors, and several have proved themselves in the professions, but these are very few. The vast majority are Reservation Indians, frustrated, hopeless and often degenerate, no longer Indian in anything except name.

There are a few tribes in the far north who still live a more or less traditional Indian life. They were either driven into this inhospitable land by the tribal wars of the past, or they retreated there before the relentless advance of the white man. They live a very different life from that now pursued by the main body of their race.

Among the Indians there are occasional millionaires and many living in abject poverty, but the true Indian has virtually disappeared. Here and there small groups, made up of one or two families, retain as much of their

119

former way of life as circumstances allow, and they owe
this to shrewd elders who foresaw what the fate of the
red man was bound to be. It is one of these groups which
I came to know, and whose members won my regard.

These Indians were related to the Bloods, and their
reserve adjoined the forest reserve. Since there had been
peace among the nations, as the chief tribes were called,
there had been an admixture of Blackfeet, Sarcees and
Crees, so that this group was fairly representative. Though
the Indians are of many nations and speak some fifty
different languages, each of which has many dialects,
they all have much in common. Only their relatives, the
Esquimos, seem to be very distinct as a people.

I established friendly and even intimate relations with
this group of Blood Indians. They had resisted the temptation to be caught in the debilitating life of the Reservation, and were in consequence preserving many of the
elements of a way of life that was thousands of years old.
This does not mean that they had not been extensively
influenced by the presence of the white man. One of
them, in fact, had taken a college education and was
known as Mr Joseph Strange, LL.B. His Indian name was
Joe Two Strange Men, and in him white culture and
Indian tradition were strongly mixed.

A full-blooded Indian, he lived as one, and was the
grandson of Lynx Paw, the chief of the tribe. Possessing
the formal education of a University graduate, he was
also steeped in the lore of the forest. In spite of this, he
frequently complained that he had lost too much time in
academic pursuits to be as competent as he desired in
the ways of nature. Significantly, he was glad to be known
as Chief Joe. Many of the white people living in Canada
and the United States look upon the Indian as dirty,
ignorant and barbarous, having obtained this impression
from the movies and lurid magazine fiction. This is the
idea which seems to prevail in other parts of the world,
although the accusation that the Indians are dirty is often
made by people who leave a beauty spot littered with
waste paper in the form of cartons, food and ice-cream

wrappers. A similar assortment may be seen around one of the Indian camps at tourist resorts, but the litter is not of the Indians, but of the tourists, although it is the Indians who clear it away.

A series of treaties have been made with the Indians since the white man found his way into the Americas and Canada, and, one after another, these treaties have been broken. But not by the Indians. Almost always they have been broken by the whites, who shamelessly robbed the red men of their lands, and herded them into reserves which progressively became smaller and smaller. Piece by piece the reserves were stolen, until in the end the Indians found themselves penned up in a corner of territory much too small for them to continue their normal way of life.

The white man, prompted by conscience, then tried to teach them his own way of life. But this was something the Indians had no wish to master and to which they were temperamentally unsuited. It is impossible to transform a race of hunters and nomads into static agriculturists in the space of two or three decades. It is equally impossible to force on such a people a religion which is so far removed from all their previous knowledge that it merely confuses. At best these well-meaning intentions could turn the red man only into poor imitations of the white man, and this, of course, is largely what has been achieved.

It must be said in fairness that, once the Department for Indian Affairs really came to grips with the problem of the red man, it effected a great improvement, and one or two Indian Agents I have met were devoting their lives to bettering the state of the people for which they were responsible. Unfortunately, the damage was done before this enlightened attitude was adopted. As a race the Indians are finished, and only a few remnants of a once splendid people cling to the ever narrowing edge of their independence.

To herd Indians into a restricted area is akin to caging an eagle. Freedom and independence were essential to their well-being. They were, indeed, vital to their life, and to subsidise them merely has the result of postponing the inevitable end. The attitude of the Indians who have accepted the life of the reserves is much like that of the imprisoned hawk, despondent and listless on his perch. They are unhappy, unhealthy and subdued.

This, of course, is the case with the older generation. The young find some satisfaction perhaps in absorbing the white man's education, and his vices. They are intelligent and remarkably quick to learn, but they still labour under the disadvantage of being Indians. They master a trade, but in the labour market, even if superior in skill to their white opposites, they are still regarded as inferior. Although this would be strenuously denied in many quarters, there is no doubt that an insidious colour bar operates. Thus, because of his circumstances, the Indian is neither one thing nor another, save in exceptional cases. And every Indian, no matter how well he adjusts himself to the situation the white man has produced, has lost something vital to his well-being, and that something can never be replaced.

In his natural state the Indian was an extraordinarily healthy creature. Sickness was a rarity, and his natural herbal remedies were sufficient to repel the ailments which overtook him. Contact with the white man, however, has changed all that. Canned and devitalised foods, lack of incentives which appeal to him, and the revolutionary change in his way of life, which occurred much too quickly, have reduced him to but a shadow of his former self.

Unable to adjust himself to the new conditions, the red man proved highly susceptible to diseases which he had never experienced before, or only very rarely. He fell victim to tuberculosis, cancer and glaucoma, as well as other complaints. The white man treated him with all the drugs and instruments of his medical science, but cures proved difficult, for the resistance of the Indians proved to be low and the will to live was often absent.

All sorts of reasons have been advanced to explain the

prevalence of disease in the reserves. At a time when glaucoma was causing an alarming amount of blindness and near blindness, I talked with an old Indian on this subject. I am inclined to think that his opinion on the matter is as sound as any I have ever heard.

" Man's body," he said, " made of what he eat and what his mother eat before he come. Sick food make body sick."

I asked Chief Joe to enlarge upon this statement the next time I met him. What he told me convinced me that the Indians had their own understanding of vitamins and what constituted a balanced diet. It appeared that they regarded canned or processed food as a lifeless and sick food, and that, I am sure, is very near the truth.

Indians were allowed to come and go in the Forest Reserve as they wished. The reserves are sanctuaries for wild life, but the treaty with the Indians allowed them to kill whatever game they liked. It says much for their honesty and great good sense that they rarely, if ever, took advantage of their privilege. It was my personal experience of them that they remained faithful to the letter of an unwritten law that the game should not be destroyed. They might occasionally take a rabbit or a spruce partridge, and even then never out of season.

Although the claim has sometimes been denied, the Indians have always been conservationists. They killed only to eat and clothe themselves, knowing that to kill within the reserve would rapidly result in complete extinction of the few remaining animals.

This conduct was in sharp contrast with that adopted by the white " sportsman." He, in fact, had to be carefully watched. The guns he carried into the reserves had to be sealed, for his creed when in the bush seemed to be summed up accurately in the phrase, " If it moves shoot it." So much was this the attitude that, in the hunting season, it was necessary to wear something bright red in colour in order to avoid getting shot. But even this precaution was inadequate, as accidents each year ran into hundreds.

An Indian not only wishes to see the animal he is hunting, but he is intent on seeing it well enough to be able to determine what kind of an animal it is, its age and sex. He is also just as intent on shooting from such a position that a kill is virtually a certainty, while the risk of wounding is reduced to the minimum.

The Indians who frequented the Forest Reserve were unofficial, though first rate, game wardens, and they greatly helped in containing the numbers of the cougar and the wolf. Once, in the vicinity of Black Lake, I came upon a small encampment of these Indians. We exchanged the usual "Hows," and then the leader said: "Cougar around here. Him kill deer. Maybe I get him. You think so?"

I agreed that it would be a good idea to get the cougar, and get him they did. For when I returned the following day, the skin was already stretched.

Rightly the Indians were delighted, and they had no idea that they had made me feel annoyed with myself. I had been past this place a score of times during the summer, and I had seen no cougar nor even a trace of one, although I prided myself on having at least the rudiments of woodcraft. Yet these people, visiting the place for the first time, had at once spotted some track which to me had been invisible. They had followed it to a point where a deer had been killed, knew just where they would find the creature responsible, and on top of all that knew without seeing it, that the cougar was a male.

This highly specialised knowledge of the ways of the wild was something that few white men have ever mastered, and those few only after a lifetime of experience, and even then as the result of obtaining their knowledge from the Indians, under whom they served their apprenticeship.

This almost uncanny mastery of the art of woodmanship is not born with the Indian, as some people seem to imagine. It is true that generations of forebears may well have passed on the necessary temperament to acquire this type of skill, but each individual learns it only by immense concentration and acute observation.

These semi-independent families could not live entirely on the country. The game was far too scarce for that, and in order to secure the many roots, berries and herbs they needed, it was necessary to cover a vast area. The produce they needed would be plentiful in some places and not in others. Again, the wild rice which used to grow in sloughs on the prairies, and which served them as bread, was almost unobtainable, only small amounts being found in the area to which they were more or less restricted.

Thus, while a few could partially live on the country, had what was available been divided amongst the whole of the Indians, it would have been negligible. However, those who did cling to the old way as much as they could reaped the benefit in the shape of better health and enjoyed a certain feeling of independence. In winter they had to be within reasonable distance of the Indian Agency and the store, but while they made camp within the reserve they were not of it. They kept themselves to themselves, living as far as possible upon the food they had collected, smoked or dried during the summer.

I learned about a dozen or so Indian words which I have since forgotten, and I never attempted to master the language. It seems to be the habit of the Indians to take two or three words which are plentifully besprinkled with prefixes, suffixes and " infixes," link them together and make one word, so long in some cases that it took in up to a hundred letters. One Indian I knew gloried in the name of Frog-that-jumps-in-lake-and-makes-big-splash. As the Indian equivalents of " frog," " jump," " lake " and " splash " are much longer than their English renderings, the name represented no small mouthful.

This Indian told me with a twinkle in his eye that his name was the reason why he had never learned to write. Had he done so, he would have been expected to sign his name every time he visited the Indian Agent, whereas all he was required to do was make a cross. The word cross was rendered as " one-short-stick-he-lay-on-other-stick-and-point-two-ways," along with the appropriate gestures to convey exactly what he meant.

I once asked Chief Joe if all these, to us, queer names were not somewhat confusing, and he explained their origin in this way:

"At or near the birth of a child there may be some occurrence out of the ordinary, or again some incident that is quite usual. And unless the parents have already figured out a name the infant is named after whatever it was that happened. In my case two strange men came into camp, and Joe was added after a Rancher who had recently done the family a service. Such names are not duplicated within a tribe and as far as possible care is taken that they do not clash with names used in a neighbouring community with whom there is intercourse."

"There are some incidents," I said, "which can happen to many tribes at once. What about those?"

"That is true," Chief Joe agreed, "but we have always had a way of sorting them out. Supposing there is an almighty clap of thunder, and about the same time a child is born in each of two neighbouring camps. Or there may be one clap of thunder in each place. An obvious choice of name would be Big Thunder, but as soon as it became known that there were two identical names, one would be changed, maybe to Thunder that Shakes the Teepee."

"So there is no risk of confusion?" I said.

"None at all," he replied. "In fact, the Indians find your method of using surnames bewildering. For instance, I am the son of Big Thunder and Starlight, and the grandson of Lynx Paw and Willow Wand. Now there are forty odd descendants of Lynx Paw, and if we were all Lynx Paws, even though another name was added, the Indian mind would find itself confused, sorting out the Joe, Tom, Harry, Mister, Miss and Mrs Lynx Paws. To them it would be as bad as it is for you looking up a Smith in the telephone book when you are not sure of the initials."

The Indians I came to know well proved to be proud, intelligent, sensitive and independent, and when in their company I always felt self-conscious about being a member of the White Race which had treated them with such a lack of sympathy and imagination. The feeling was somewhat mitigated by the fact that I was British, and that the treatment of the Indians had been far better in Canada than it had been below the 49th parallel. During the last phases of the wars against the red man, many Indians had sought sanctuary in Canada, knowing the harsh treatment they would have received had they remained south of the border.

There was one occasion during this particular summer when I paid a visit to an Indian camp which had an atmosphere about it that was different from anything I had ever experienced. It was as much like an Indian encampment of a hundred years ago as one is likely to find today. At some places such as Banff the Indians put on a camp and sun dance for the benefit of the tourists, but this type of show is simply an annual travesty of the real thing. The Indians have no heart in it, and take part only because it is a means of augmenting their meagre incomes. At these yearly shows the red men sell "Indian" beaded buckskins, and other kinds of bric-à-brac beloved of the tourists. But the only work done on most of these articles by the Indians is the removal of the stamp or ticket which betrays one of Canada's large mail order houses. I have no doubt that the Indians would be pleased to make these things themselves, but although the beads are readily obtainable, the buckskin isn't. So the good old cow is called on to fill the gap.

I first had knowledge of the genuine Indian camp when a party of Indians passed my cabin at Wind Lake, one of whom was Chief Joe.

"I was hoping I might find you here or on the trail," he said. "It saves me a trip."

"What's on your mind, Chief?" I asked him.

"I wanted to let you know that there will be quite a crowd of us in your district for a few days," he told me. "Many more than usual. There is to be a bit of a Pow-Wow, a ceremony that comes around only once in a while. After that a dozen or so will stay on fishing, as usual."

He gave no hint as to what the ceremony was about, and it would have been discourteous to ask. In any case, the need to do so was dispelled by what he said next.

"My father, Big Thunder, will be presiding," he told me, "and he invites you to visit us. Perhaps you could pay us an official visit on Saturday and stay over Sunday."

This was rather formal for Chief Joe, but his mention of a specific time for the visit made it plain that they had no wish to be disturbed before then.

"Please tell Big Thunder," I said, "that I shall be honoured to visit him on Saturday, and, if nothing urgent calls for my attention, I shall be happy to stay until Sunday."

Chief Joe relaxed. He had been unwilling to ask me outright to avoid their camp during a particular period, and now that the matter was settled he became as friendly and informal as usual.

"It will be worth your while to come," he said. "This is to be a one hundred per cent Indian camp, and you will see us in a new setting."

"Where is it to be?" I asked.

Chief Joe smiled.

"You had better let me know what time to expect you," he said. "Then I will meet you at the big balsam about half a mile this side of the Sikanaska River. That will guard against you having difficulty in finding us."

I knew there were a few balsam trees down that way, but I was unwilling to admit that I could not remember such a tree at the point he had mentioned. Therefore, I said :

"Don't say my woodcraft is so bad I can't see where something like a hundred horses have gone to."

He laughed heartily at that. He had taught me a little of the art of tracking, often twitting me when I failed to see some small sign that was right under my nose.

"I only suggested that you might have some difficulty," he said. "You see, we have no intention of advertising our whereabouts, as we have no wish to attract uninvited guests."

The following Saturday, just before reaching the rendezvous, I noticed many tracks which had been made by horses as they came from the opposite direction. As they did not continue beyond the point where I had first noticed them it was obvious that they had left the trail somewhere. It seemed sensible to assume that, if a number of horses branch off, there must be a very clear track where they did so. But there was no such track.

This could only mean that they had left the trail in ones and twos, yet there appeared to be but few places where a horse could have gone far from the trail without being brought to a halt by a tangle of windfalls.

As soon as I saw it I remembered the balsam Chief Joe had mentioned, and took myself to task for failing to do so before. I suppose the advantage lies with the Indians because, while I had to remember details, they had every inch of the country in which they travelled " photographed " on their mind, though they had travelled that way but seldom.

I almost jumped out of my skin when a voice beside me said: " You are right on time."

And there, seated on a windfall within a few feet of the trail, was Chief Joe.

" You should have seen me," he said. " Although I did not scare your horse, he spotted me some way back."

We both laughed.

Noticing me eyeing his handsome apparel, he said: " You have seen nothing yet. Wait until you see some of the others."

He led me to where his horse was hidden. There was no visible trail and it was impossible to travel in a straight line for more than a few yards. Looking magnificent in the full panoply of a minor Chief, he mounted and led me along a winding maze. Here and there I could see that a windfall which could not be surmounted had been cunningly cut away so that it was barely noticeable. The trail, such as it was, was not marked in any way and had I had to follow it alone I should have found myself retracing my steps many times.

Having travelled about a mile, we came to a point where several trails of the type we had followed converged, and from then on I was much more certain of the way.

The Indians had camped at one of those places which, seen from a distance, do not betray their real nature. When coming over a high point on the trail from Black Lake it appeared to be all forest stretching back into a " bay " where the mountain range curved. There was, apparently, nowhere to go and nothing to attract tourists. Consequently no trail had been cut, and only if there had been a fire in the vicinity would I or anybody else have had reason to go there.

There was a swampy clearing of about twenty acres, but it was not muskeg, as over a hundred horses grazed upon it. On higher ground beside a little creek that flowed into the swamp was the camp which was so large that it resembled a village, made up of colourful teepees. I was met by four Indian Chiefs magnificently attired in beautifully beaded buckskins and feathered headdresses, each feather tipped with horsehair. Each carried across one arm a medicine bag made of otter or some other fine skin and embellished with a wonderfully designed beaded piece of pure white leather, like a stole.

I soon realised that I was being treated as a Very Important Person. Not only was I the one white man to visit the camp, but all the finery had been retained especially for my benefit, as the ceremony was already ended.

I soon learnt why I had been accorded this favoured treatment. It was not because I was the Ranger of the district. Due to my frequent talks with Chief Joe, his grandfather Chief Lynx Paw had been apprised of the fact that I was not one of those white men who considered the Indians to be merely ignorant savages.

" My father, Big Thunder," said Chief Joe simply, and the most resplendent of the four, a tall, high-featured

Indian, his grave face full of character, stepped forward and shook hands.

"You are welcome," he said. "Chief Lynx Paw, the head of my people, knows of you, but he can no more travel so far or he would welcome you himself."

I was then introduced to the three other chiefs. My horse was taken by a pretty, smiling little girl, and for a few moments I surveyed my surroundings. The teepees decorated with Indian paintings no doubt recorded some of the history of the people, but I was unable to understand them. Many of them were made of canvas, but some of them were cherished heirlooms made of split buffalo hide.

A few children played, laughing quietly at times, but their play was not punctuated by screams and raucous cries. Everyone was gaily dressed, all was trim and tidy, and while the camp had been there only three days and would be gone on the morrow, it somehow exuded an air of orderly permanence. I had the feeling that I was a usurper, and that these were the real Canadians. I suppose it was inevitable that the white man should sooner or later occupy this lovely country, but I could not help wishing that it had been done with greater grace and understanding.

I stayed overnight, and that evening quite a pow-wow was held in the teepee of Big Thunder, attended by the four Chiefs, Chief Joe and myself. The flickering shadows cast by the fire in the centre made the grave rugged features of the elders look as if they had been carved from rock. I felt that I might well have been one of the old *voyageurs* of a century before.

Chief Joe had already said to me: "Ask them anything you wish to know. They love to talk, especially about old times. You will hear much that you know already, but their way of telling it will give you an insight into the Indian mind."

The moment an opportunity occurred, I said to Big Thunder: "It is a great honour for me, a white man, to be here. I know full well that your people have suffered

ST9*

much at the hands of the white man in the past, but what do you think could have been done to have made things better?"

Big Thunder grunted and solemnly nodded his fine head, the other Chiefs adding their grunts and nods. Then he said:

" Life for the Indians came to an end when the buffalo was finished. Two countries took part in that, Canada and the United States. I will speak of Canada, where my people have mostly lived for many generations. Chief White Hawk, who is of the Blackfeet, can tell you better than me what happened in the south."

White Hawk, a fine old man of at least eighty, who had travelled some two hundred miles for this gathering, grunted expressively.

" In Canada," Big Thunder said, " first came a good white man. Like us, these first comers lived by hunting, and a few of them were traders. With these we could share our land, for they killed sparingly, knowing that it was mad to destroy that on which they depended for their lives. They were men of their word, and we could treat with them in confidence. If one of them did wrong he was punished as swiftly by his fellow white men as by the Indians.

" Then came a great many men who were mad, without sense at all. Behind them came steel (the railway) bringing countless numbers more. All seemed to be mad. The Indians could not stop them by force, for they were too many and too well armed, and their own rulers could not control them. More buffalo were killed in a month for their hides—the meat being left to rot and waste—than the Indians would have needed in a whole summer.

" Then came a hard winter, and the buffalo went far to the south. There were still many left, and we expected them to return the following year. But they never came back. Other game, such as the deer and moose, began to get scarce. In the end we were forced to trap beaver— the little talking people—and trade with the posts in order to live. We did not like trapping beaver, and some, although they starved, never did trap beaver. But the mad men caught them in thousands and thousands. Even the beaver with young, or heavy with young were taken in the spring when they were easy to trap. The first trappers did not do this. They caught beaver, but always left some in every lodge so that there would be more.

" It became too late to organise a big war against these people. We lost all that meant life to us, but if that was the wish of the Great Spirit, who am I to dispute it?"

Big Thunder had spoken without hate or bitterness, being content simply to sum up the facts.

" But you asked," he resumed, " what could the white man have done better. That I do not know, although he could not have done much worse. To have left the Indians enough buffalo and enough land for them to find grass would have meant leaving to us much of Canada and much of the United States. So, when the Indian way of life was no longer possible, white men with good intentions wished to turn us into white men. They thought only as white men, and could not see that the Indians were different.

" It is like this. At Wainwright there is a herd of buffalo. The white man, as soon as he had controlled those of his own kind without brains, saved a few buffalo and they have increased. But they are not buffalo. They are tame creatures like a cow. If they were allowed to go wild and were not given hay in winter, they would starve. They would not even know how to follow the grass to the south if they could do so. They are soft and tame. So, too, with the Indian. He has been given food and has not had to hunt. He, too, has become soft and tame. Many could no longer keep themselves alive even if there was game and they were free to hunt it.

" But Indians are not buffalo, and evil has overtaken them. The young men have become soft in mind as well as in body, and have learnt many of the white man's faults. Many girls no longer take pride in their virtue. We have been given schools where we may learn the white man's ways, and we have lost the learning of the Indians.

We have been given tools to grow food on land that is no good to the white man for such a purpose. We who have been hunters from the beginning!

"No. I say the Indian is finished. Maybe those mad ones would have killed us all, but others did not allow it. I think the white man could have done no more than he has done, however, any more than the mind of the Indian can be changed. We old ones are grateful to have lived as long as the Great Spirit intended. As you see here, some of us have managed to preserve a little of our old life. In many generations there will be no Indians, only white men. Many people come from many races to this country, and all become Canadians. So will it be with us. The white man, in the end, will make us as one with him.

"The happy hunting grounds and a new life wait for us who cannot be changed. We shall soon travel the Spirit Trail. I have spoken."

Big Thunder's oration called for a chorus of approving grunts.

After I had assured the Chief that his remarks appealed to me as sound in reasoning and scrupulous in fairness, White Hawk took up the tale.

In spite of his grave aspect, he had a sense of humour.

"What Big Thunder has spoken," he said, "is true, too, of the peoples to the south. But I think we had more of what he calls the mad men. We knew from the early days that the white man was bound to win in the end, but there were many battles. We were ready to come to reasonable terms, and treaties were made with those I call the good men who made the white man's laws. But these laws were set aside, and the Indians fought in the hope that something would be done by those in the east to avoid further bloodshed. But it was not so. The news that was taken to the east was that of liars.

"It was natural for the Indians to fight for the lands that were their life. White men have done the same, even quite recently. But this I want you to know. The Indian was said to be simply a cruel and heartless savage. When he won a battle, which was not often, it was called a massacre, but when the white man won it was called a victory. We were never understood by those who were far from us, and those nearer said that the only good Indian was a dead one. I have no complaint about that, because we said just the same about the white man, and I was responsible for making many white men good ones."

Here Chief White Hawk allowed himself the ghost of a smile, and there were grunts from the others which might well have been chuckles.

"Sometimes," the Chief resumed, "the white soldiers had victories where whole tribes, including the women and children, were killed. The Indians did the same thing. There is a white man's saying that two wrongs do not make a right. But when men are angry they are all savages. There was a time, as you know, when General Custer hoped to catch a certain band of Sioux Indians and punish them for their misdeeds. That was the time when many nations of Indians had an alliance, and I was a Chief of one section of the Blackfeet who took part in that battle. We caught Custer. Had we lost the battle I, for one, knew I should be hanged, and I don't think Custer expected to be invited to tea if he lost. Well, the result was a 'massacre.'

"Now, let me tell of something else. There is a place not more than three days journey from here where lie the bones of a whole tribe of Blackfeet, my people. I was away hunting at the time or I should not be here today. There was a white man who had a farm near our camp. He interfered with the Indian women, and one day he raped one of them. And when the husband protested, the white man attacked and badly injured him. He was very angry and, a few days later, he killed the man who had wronged his wife. Maybe you might have done the same?"

I had to agree that, under such circumstances, such a reprisal was very much of a possibility.

"But the killing," Chief White Hawk said, "was against the white man's law. So, before dawn, soldiers crept up on the camp and fired into the teepees while the Indians slept. The people ran out and my father tried to reason with the soldiers, but he died, and every other person in the camp died with him. The teepees were piled in a heap and the bodies of my people were burned with them. It was said that the Blackfeet had rebelled, and that there had been a battle in which the soldiers had been victorious."

The white man, alas, often displayed his savagery, and there was a famous instance of this at Sand Creek, Colorado, in 1864. The Indians were in a state of unrest because efforts were being made to dislodge them from lands they had been given in the Treaty of 1851. The Governor sent word that the White Father was angry, but, being kindly and just, he would overlook the misdeeds of the Indians, supply them with provisions and show them a place of safety if they surrendered. Some five hundred did surrender to the Agent at Fort Lyon, and set up an encampment at Sand Creek. But the Rev John M. Chivington, Colonel of the 3rd Colorado Cavalry, was out for Indian blood. One day at dawn, the unsuspecting Indians were massacred by Chivington's men. Afterwards, he reported with great satisfaction that there were no prisoners and no survivors.

Serious trouble followed. The Arapaho, Sioux, Cheyenne and Apaches all had tribal members in the Sand Creek massacre, and they went on the warpath. There followed a year of bloodshed before peace came once more to the plains.

" I tell you these things," White Hawk said, " because I want you to know it was not always the Indians who were wrong. Chief Big Thunder has already told you of the winter when the buffalo did not return to the north. That was because the plains in the south were black with their dead bodies, and the stench from their carcases was in the air a day's journey from where they lay. They were worth a dollar each for their hides, and about another dollar for their tongues. That was how the white man saw these herds of countless thousands of buffalo. They were worth so many easy dollars to him. And because of that they destroyed herds which could not be replaced in hundreds of years, only a few stragglers escaping.

" But it is all over now. It had to be, and I now count many white men as my friends, and we are at peace."

A smile flickered on all the faces round the fire when one of the other Chiefs, whose name I have forgotten, said, " Too much peace not good for a man."

The talk went on for a long time, and when religion was mentioned, I seized the opportunity to ask Big Thunder what his attitude was to this difficult problem.

" I am converted to silence," he answered, his face expressionless. " When the pastor calls I am Christian; when he has gone I am Indian."

The next day, within an hour of the camp coming to life, all the fine raiment had been stored away in skin bags, all save three or four teepees were packed, and they were ready to move. I said goodbye to the Chiefs and thanked them. I also sent my regards to Chief Lynx Paw, who, being over ninety, had to stay on the reserve where some of the family were always on hand to see to his needs. I would have very much liked to meet the old chap, but I never had that good fortune.

After breakfast and a stroll, most of the day was spent in Chief Joe's teepee talking; while those who remained for the fishing set up racks for the drying and smoking of the fish which the Indians have employed, perhaps for thousands of years.

"There's still more I would like to know about the Indian people," I said to Chief Joe.

"What, in particular?" he asked.

"I would be interested to hear your opinion on the origins of the Indian race," I said. "Why they appear to have such a mental superiority, and why they appear to have progressed to a certain point and then advanced no farther."

Chief Joe laughed.

"You say we are mentally superior," he said. "But to whom do you think we are superior?"

"I am speaking generally," I replied. "You have demonstrated your intelligence by taking a degree at college. But all the Indians I have met, and especially those who retain the traditional ways of their race as much as they are able, reveal themselves as deep and intelligent thinkers. The Chiefs last night revealed that, but an ordinary Indian, like old Tom Dusty Face, for instance, betrays the same quality. They all seem to possess the same power of logical reasoning. There are few, if any, morons among them, although most are illiterate. Yet in all the countries where there is national and compulsory education the vast majority of the people have no literary pursuits, being content with nothing more than the tabloid press and comic strips."

Chief Joe chuckled and nodded.

"The answer is quite simple," he said. "In the past, the Indian had to be smart in order to survive. It was no use leaving it to the next man to do the thinking. Each man had to size up a situation and make his own decision. That is a habit of mind which remains with those who still try to preserve the old way of life. Unfortunately, you'll find quite a number of morons amongst the youngsters on the reserve.

"Some years ago, when I was full of academic enthusiasm, I tried to persuade an uncle of mine, a very wise old bird, to learn to read. He would have none of it and maintained that it would spoil his brain.

"'I am educated in my way,' my uncle said. 'When I want to know something I think and find out. If I read other men's thoughts, they think for me. Maybe they think right, maybe wrong. I do not know which, so I still have to think for myself. If a man fills his head with more than it can hold, many good thoughts will spill out and be lost.'"

"There seems to be something in what your uncle said," I remarked.

"I think so, too," Chief Joe agreed. "The Indian is intensely practical, and would not be amused by the man who tried to explain to him that there are occasions when two and two make five. As for the origins of the Indian people, we have only theories. Our history extends deep into the past, and a body of legend has been handed down by word of mouth over thousands of years.

"Once, I asked Lynx Paw the same question, and I fear he regarded it as stupid. For all he said was, 'We were put here by the Great Spirit to wait and learn how to live until we go to the other life.' And maybe he was right. For I find it hard to accept theories that would explain the race as originating in fishermen who hailed from Japan, China or Malaya."

"That doesn't strike me as very probable, either," I said.

"Fishermen might have been blown to these shores in the Atlantic," Chief Joe said. "But they would have perished without issue unless they brought women with them. And what would women be doing in European or African fishing boats? It may be true that there was a time when Africa and America were joined, but that must have been long before man arrived on the scene at all. In any case, had we hailed from Africa, we should be negroid, and we are not."

"No," I said. "You have very different physical charac-

teristics from nation to nation, but there is no trace of the
negroid to be found in any Indians that I know."

"That is so," Chief Joe replied. "We differ in appearance from the stately Iroquois to the squat Esquimo, and
in colour from tan to a near black. Nevertheless, the main
body of our race have aquiline features and their skin is
of a reddish tint. Red Indians is an apt description. But
why red? In other parts of the world there are white,
black, brown and yellow, and plenty of shades of all of
them. Yet the only red men in the world are found here.
That seems to indicate that we spring from no other race.
And that is further borne out by the fact that, although
we are many nations, we all have much in common in
customs, religion and dress.

"The Esquimo, who is not red skinned, although he is
classed as an Indian, has the appearance of a Mongolian.
Perhaps he did arrive on these coasts by accident. They
remain faithful to the coast, and seem unable to adapt
themselves to anything else. They were probably fishermen from the orient, who took their families with them
on their fishing expeditions. That might explain how they
succeeded in founding a new race. But the claim that
other seafaring races reached this country in the same
way seems to me to have little to support it.

"Of course, it cannot be denied that there has been
some infiltration from many lands. We have a few individuals with a distinctly slant-eyed cast of countenance.
This might be due to inland Mongols from Siberia crossing the ice of the Bering Straits in winter and penetrating
inland. Here and there traces of other races can be
detected. I often think my father, when seen in the fire-
light as he was last night, could be a sculptured bust of
Julius Caesar himself. Besides, some of our customs and
beliefs seem to be connected with the orient.

"The Indians speak some fifty different languages, but
that is hardly surprising. Even with a written record a
language suffers considerable changes over the years. And
when there is no written record, anything can happen to
a language in a very short time."

" What of your own nation?" I asked. " Can you throw any light on its history?"

" It is fairly easy to trace the Algonquin nation to which we Bloods belong," he said. " It originated in the far east of the country, and it seems to me reasonable enough that, before that, the people who established it made their way from the south as the climate improved. They brought with them many of our present-day customs and collected an admixture of foreign blood en route. But, after all, there is much in common between us and the Sioux and Comanche, to name only three nations, all of which were widely separated.

" Therefore, I am inclined to think that the red man originated right here in North America. Such prehistoric creatures as the diplodocus and the triceratops did, so why shouldn't the Indians have done the same thing?"

In the course of our discussion of Indian customs, the traditional initiation rites were mentioned. These rites have often been used as evidence of the barbarity of the red man, but I felt sure there must be much more in them than plain sadism.

" There is much more in them than that," Chief Joe said. " They tie up in a way with religious beliefs. They are forbidden now, but even if that were not the case, the rites would have died, for they would have lost their use. As you heard my father say last night, the young men have become soft. That includes me, I suppose, for I have no wish to be initiated, although, had I been born a few decades earlier, I should have taken it as a matter of course.

" The custom arose out of the belief that it was neces- sary for a young man to prove that he was the master of his body, and that his spirit was in control. A Brave was subjected to very severe tests to prove this, and if he failed he was regarded as of very small account. All the Chiefs who were here last night have been subjected to initiation rites. Perhaps you noticed that one or two little fingers were missing, and in Big Thunder's case part of another finger as well. I have often seen my father's scars, and they were clearly the result of harsh wounds."

"The Spartans subjected their children to physical ordeals," I said. "They thought it was good for them."

"Ah, yes," said Chief Joe. "But the candidates for initiation to manhood were all volunteers. No one was forced to take part, but any youth who refused lost all rights to take part in what were regarded as manly occupations. For instance, he received no share of the spoils of war, and any girl who looked after him did so contemptuously.

"The candidate first fasted for four days and nights, and not a drop of water was allowed to pass his lips. Thus, when the real test began, he was not feeling by any means fit, although the lack of food and liquid had its practical value in that it prevented excessive bleeding.

"Then, in the presence of the Chiefs and the rest of the tribe, the candidates proved their right to be known as Men or Braves. The Master of Ceremonies pinched up a piece of flesh on the breast, made a hole with a sharp knife and inserted a wooden skewer. This was repeated on the other breast, on the shoulders and thighs. The number of the incisions varied from tribe to tribe, but the average was about six.

"Rawhide thongs were then fastened to the skewers of the chest and shoulders and the victim was suspended from the top of a lodge so that his feet barely touched the ground. To the thigh skewers were fastened such items as a buffalo skull or a shield. The drums started and there was a mad dance to endeavour to break away from the suspending thongs. On no account were the skewers to be withdrawn endways. They had to be torn out through the flesh. When free the other skewers received attention. Of course several youths took part at the same time, giving to the ceremony the element of competition.

"The Chiefs were all the time noting how often a candidate fainted, and how long he took to recover and continue the rites. Thus this, to us, shocking ordeal lasted a considerable time. And as soon as a youth was free of his skewers he could go to where the tomahawk and block waited and there have the little finger of his left hand chopped off or if very ambitious he could offer a joint off the next. Then he could have a drink, and it's my opinion he would be more than ready for it.

"The youth having attested his bravery, the Chiefs knew to whom they could entrust the most delicate and dangerous missions. They knew who would be least likely to disgrace the tribe should they die unpleasantly at the hands of an enemy."

"I'm inclined to think you have grown a bit soft, Joe," I said.

He laughed and nodded.

"I must admit that the Indians have been a disappointment in some respects," he said. "Compared with many primitive peoples we reached a high stage of advancement. Then we quit. It seems that little has changed in a thousand years except for the introduction of horses and guns. Yet when some learned whites adapted our phonetics to the alphabet, some Indians, after the system had been explained to them, were able to read in a matter of weeks. Others took longer, but it was evident that the Indians had been capable of developing a written language long ago. Yet they never took the trouble to do so.

"The Indians could see no immediate use for a written language. There was plenty to do; they were always on the move and, from a practical point of view, they had all that they required. The Indians are intensely independent and practical, and their education took the form of a knowledge of the ways of the wilds. They developed this knowledge to such a degree that it virtually ranks as a science.

"Their methods of working smoothly as a team when setting up camp, so that, even in winter snows, they were so settled in within an hour that they might have been there ages; their ingenious traps; their methods of making clothes and preserving food, revealed in these things a superiority which left the white man astonished and helpless. To the Indian mind that was enough.

"When the horse made its appearance, they instantly saw its advantages. Soon they were superior as horsemen to those who had introduced the animal. And their methods of horse training were superior also. The Indian refused to be encumbered with a saddle and bridle. He demanded full freedom of movement, the horse being guided by the pressure of a knee, the hands being at liberty to employ the bow and arrow, and, later, the rifle.

"The same thing happened with guns. Previously it had not been found necessary to improve on the bow, as it was very efficient. But as soon as the advantage of the rifle was noted, it took only a short time for the Indians, generally, to become better marksmen than the whites.

"The game in our country was so plentiful that we needed to seek no other form of main supply. The game, however, did not stay in one place all the time, and so we became nomadic hunters, adjusting ourselves to that kind of life, and the adaptation needed no little intelligence.

"To attain the specialised knowledge we acquired called for an intelligence as high as any displayed by the white man. And for successive generations to learn the accumulated knowledge of the Indians required at least as much in the way of learning as does the average education of the 'civilised' world. Had we been static and needed towns, I'm sure we could have built them. And I'm quite sure we could have satisfied any practical need which had called for our attention.

"Our laws were strict, and they worked well. It is true that the form of Government was very local, but it was also exceedingly democratic. Chieftainship was not necessarily hereditary. Normally a son followed his father, providing he displayed the qualities regarded as necessary to the office. But a Chief who showed that he lacked the necessary character and ability was not allowed to maintain his position. Nor was a Chief a despot whose word could not be challenged. If it was felt that he was wrong in any decision he made, the matter was put to

the vote, and if the vote went against the Chief he
accepted it without question.

" Before the white man established his trading posts,
the Indians knew nothing of commerce. All the raw
materials they needed were to hand, and their methods of
manufacture satisfied them in every way. There was no
point in producing a surplus, for that would have meant
having to carry it about. They diverged from the strictly
practical only in the decorating of their clothes and
teepees, and their decorations all had meaning and did
not add to the problems of transport.

" So a comparison of the Indian of a hundred years ago
with the majority of white men of today reveals, generally speaking, more ignorance amongst Europeans than
was to be found in the red man. Perhaps, then, we can
say that the Indians achieved a state of development in
which they were highly satisfied, and saw no good reason
to effect any improvements."

The lunch I had that day with Chief Joe was an Indian
meal put on for my benefit. It consisted entirely of Indian
food. There were biscuits or scones made of wild rice,
broiled trout, a sort of fruit salad of blueberries, strawberries, and something like rhubarb, sweetened with wild
honey, and tea. The tea was made from a sort of sage,
and had a taste and aroma rather like some herbal in-
fusion used for inhaling. But once the taste had been
acquired it would be as acceptable as China tea, but
having more body.

The meal was tasty and satisfying, and was produced
without any outlay. And I sat regretting a past which
seemed to contain some quite needless and terrible mistakes. Had the Indians been left sufficient buffalo, plus
enough land over which to roam, then they might well
have been an asset instead of a liability. As it is, the greedy
cropping of huge stretches of the prairies has denuded
the land of its humus to such an extent that large areas
have become a dust bowl, of no value to either the white
or red man.

As I intended to return to Wind Lake before dark there

was little time for further talk. But Chief Joe was eager
to explain the Indian attitude to religion.

"Every religion," he said, "claims that it is the only
true religion, and the Indians feel that their religion is
the truest of them all. Having been brought into contact
with the Christian religion and the various denominations
which claim to represent it, they have reacted in their
typically practical manner.

"Big Thunder is representative in this sense. He has
had many discussions with well-intentioned missionaries.
A parson from the Church of England once approached
him, and Big Thunder listened gravely and courteously,
saying not a word until the parson had finished his
explanation. Then, much to the good man's discomfiture,
he asked: 'What has the white man done that he needs
to speak to his god through a middleman?' The same
thing happens with Roman Catholics, Methodists and
others, and the same performance is repeated. Then Big
Thunder says: 'You seem to have many ways of
approaching God. It confuses me. Maybe God is confused, too, eh!' And so it went on until, as Big Thunder
himself says, he is converted to silence.

"There is no Indian religion in the accepted sense.
That is, it is in no way organised, and to call it sun
worship is a fallacy. The Indian believes in an omnipotent
mind which he calls the Great Spirit. The sun is regarded
worthy of veneration because it is the instrument and
source of all life, and that is a scientific fact.

"The Indians believe that they have two bodies, the
earthly one being used as long as required and being
discarded when the Great Spirit sees fit. That, it seems,
measures up to most other beliefs. The Indian, however,
unlike the devotees of many other religions, does not fear
God. Quite the reverse. Some claim that they are constantly in direct contact with Him, and all believe that
the Great Spirit is present in all nature. According
to the Indians, even animals and trees have some form of
spiritual body. They believe this so thoroughly that they
rarely cut down a living tree, and some old ones are

regarded as sacred. An Indian will often apologise silently to a creature he is about to kill. And after he has slain it he will stroke its face and offer further apologies. He has treated the beaver in particular always with the greatest respect. He referred to beavers as the little talking people, and some Indians claimed to be able to converse with them. They were held in such esteem by certain tribes that a man would starve and even die before taking the life of one of these creatures.

"Some individuals in every tribe have practised spiritual meditation, in much the same way as the oriental yogi. This habit of meditation began, it seems, thousands of years ago. It is claimed by one adept that he can leave his body, and travel not only to distant places but backwards and forwards in time as well.

"That may be an exaggeration, but the fact remains that in these periods of meditation, cold, heat and flies have no effect on the subject. What is more, some very accurate and useful information is obtained during these periods of prolonged reflection. An uncle of mine is an adept at these things. Usually he confines his travels or visions, or whatever they are, to forecasting what the weather will be over long or short periods, where game is to be found, and when fish are to be obtained and where. Once he told me that, during a spell of meditation, he had visited a large city in the east. This I took to mean New York, for he spoke of man-made mountains, people rushing about like ants and apparently doing nothing, while they looked at the ground and never once glanced at the sky. He stated that he could see no contentment in living in such a fashion."

Much the wiser for my experiences and conversation, I bade Chief Joe goodbye and returned to Wind Lake.

It was obvious that to get to know the Indians it was essential to live with them. They were reticent at casual meetings, and to judge them as a race from what could be observed on the reservation was almost certain to lead to false conclusions.

It is said that the Indian leaves his refuse on a camp

ST10*

site. Perhaps he does, and so do white people. In their normal circumstances, however, the Indians occupied a camp for but a short time and they were not likely to use it again for a considerable period. In the meantime nature's scavengers cleaned it up. In winter when a camp was occupied for some months, frost prevented any unpleasantness. Fresh snow covered the refuse dump from time to time, and far from being dirty it was quite sterile. The camp moved before the warm days arrived and at once the coyote and fox, and perhaps bears, saw to the cleaning up. In a short time all that remained would be a few cleanly picked bones.

It is difficult to support the claim that the Indians are ignorant. Maybe they could not read our books, but they could read something much more difficult. They could read the messages of the wild. And while they could not write, they could leave announcements and notices the white man could not see, much less could he decipher them. The Indians revealed themselves to me as shrewd, logical and certainly not in the least credulous. Indeed, they were by no means as superstitious as the European who thinks thirteen an unlucky number or who regards it as the most evil of omens to break a mirror or to open an umbrella in the house.

Perhaps there is some truth in the accusation that the Indians are savages. But where brutality and inhumanity are concerned the civilisations of America, Europe, Asia, and Africa, both in war and peace, have much to stain their records, and none can look back even into the last twenty years without a sense of shame.

The Indians are often accused of being a warlike race. The whites, unfortunately, seem to have peace merely as an interlude between wars, and it must be remembered that the tribal warfare of the Indians was generally limited to mere raiding. The object was the acquisition of spoils, and killing or getting killed was coincidental and arose mostly out of self-defence.

Poaching on one another's preserves often caused the offended tribe to take to the warpath. But it was the entire male adult population which went to war. There were no armchair generals and no reserved occupations. Everyone from the Chief down was liable to take part. And each side showed its regard for the other by all the braves wearing their best. This was done to ensure that the enemy, if he killed you, got something for his trouble. That, it seems, was a touch of chivalry not unworthy of the Knights of King Arthur.

The contestants had all been through the initiation ceremony and did not regard a scalping here and there as a very serious business. Penalties arising from being captured by the opposite side were accepted as normal procedure, and the pains were borne with equanimity and fortitude.

It would be foolish to attempt to deny that some of the Indian practices in war were inexcusable. But excesses in war are universal, and in this the Indians were showing themselves as no more or no less human than many peoples and nations who regard themselves as far superior to the red man.

But in their treatment of animals the record of Indians is stainless. Here they shame almost every other type and breed of men. The Indians were kind to animals when the Europeans regarded such an attitude as a weakness. The Indians would go to incredible lengths to ensure that a wounded animal did not creep away to die a slow, agonising death. The Indians, though they enjoyed the hunt, never killed for " sport." An Indian who would pit his skill against an angry bison bull, would do so alone, ready to take the consequences of losing, but he would be sick with disgust at an organised bull fight. No Indian would have dreamed of hunting a tame deer or of coursing a hare that was not on its own ground with an even chance of escaping. The unthinking and often deliberate cruelty that persists in a thousand backyards and hole in the corner smallholdings, or lingers in markets and the transport of animals in this and other " civilised " countries, would be looked upon by the Indians as a form of barbarism and ignorant savagery.

The Indian, in fact, has much to commend him, and his faults appear to be much too universal for them to be described as peculiar to the red man. It is true that there is room for improvement, but there are few Europeans, Americans or Canadians who have any right to tell the Indian that. For in this respect they all live in very brittle glass houses.

IX: WHEREIN I LOSE A NOSE

IT HAPPENED next winter that Lady cut her leg on some barbed wire. When the time came to journey to Wind Lake I did not regard her as fit enough to make the trip. I knew she would hate being left behind, but I arranged with a neighbour that she should run with his horses and would not want for company.

To take Lady's place I acquired a dark bay filly. She was broken to the saddle and made no undue fuss about being packed. Although she was in foal, once I was set up for the summer I could dispense with her services for a few weeks, and I anticipated no trouble. The man from whom I bought her could not say when the event would take place, but from her appearance I assumed it was some months away.

I took her with me and gave her a light load. She achieved all that I had hoped for, even to chumming up with Barney and to some extent with Paint. Being young, she was a bit skittish and full of life, and I named her Minx.

At the beginning of July, the foal seemed rather nearer than I had expected, and I stopped using the mare. She still came along with the others, however, wherever we went, trotting along behind without even a halter, and she was always on hand when the ration of oats was dished out.

That morning I was at Wind Lake. I went to fetch in the horses as usual, to find that Minx was missing. It was obvious that she had gone off to some quiet spot to have her foal. Although I'd a good idea where she would be, I did not look for her, figuring that she would show up later. Catching Barney and Paint, I took them into the little barn that Wind Lake boasted, gave them their oats, and then got my breakfast.

I had planned a trip for the day, but before leaving I took a small pan of oats and went out to see if I could locate Minx. At the place where the horses were usually found I called and rattled the oat can, but the mare did not appear. Deciding to look a bit farther, I walked along just within the timber where it edged the grassy flat. It was pretty dense, and just the sort of place the horse would choose to hide for the important occasion.

At a point where the horses had made quite a trail, going there frequently to avoid the flies in the heat of the day, I stopped and called again. Then, shaking the oat tin, I ventured a little way into the timber. I had made up my mind to go no farther, as time was getting on and Minx should foal without any assistance.

Then there was a whinny which held a strange note, and it seemed fairly certain that the foal had been born. Minx appeared from among the dense trees, coming towards me at a trot. Her ears were back, she was shaking her head and she wasn't looking at all friendly. I was not particularly concerned by her manner. We knew each other by this time and we got on well together. Besides, she had a habit of looking like this, and she had never given any sign that it was more than play. Certainly, all the time I'd had her, she had never been vicious.

I held out the oats. She quickened her pace, and it was not until she was almost upon me that I realised that she was not in a playful mood. She was angry and meant business. I tried to slip aside, but it was too late. Rearing,

she struck me in the chest, throwing me flat on my back.

Slightly winded, I could see her reared above me, her eyes savage, the hoofs coming down at me again. I rolled aside and managed to avoid the full force of the blow. Even so, the hard hoofs with eight hundred pounds behind them, hurt plenty. Once more Minx brought her hoofs down on me, giving me no time to regain my feet or scramble out of the way. How many times I half dodged the murderous blows I do not know. Probably the rearing horse was above me no more than a few seconds, but to me it seemed more like an age. I can still remember the occasion vividly, and recall that the thought passed through my mind that I could not stand the treatment much longer. I even remember seeing her feet descending upon me, and thanking providence that they were not shod.

I got to my knees and looked over my shoulder to see where the next blow was coming from. But Minx, instead of using her hoofs, was making a grab at me with her teeth. My face was right in her wide open jaws. I snatched my head back, but too late. Her teeth closed on my face, skidded off my cheekbones, taking some of the skin with them and closed on the end of my nose. There was a sound rather like that experienced when a dentist gives a twist to a tooth, and in that second I knew that a large part of my nose had gone. Curiously, the thought flashed through my mind that the loss was of no consequence, as I should not need it again. I was convinced that I was finished.

The tattoo Minx had drummed on me with her hoofs and the bite had taken almost all the fight out of me, and I was becoming quite dizzy. It was then that I heard the furious barking of a dog. At the same moment Minx's attacks on me ceased. The dog, a small one, belonged to some anglers camped by the lake. Out on a foraging trip of his own, he had evidently heard the disturbance and decided to investigate. His arrival could not have been more timely. I was no longer able to defend myself and the horse would have savaged me until it wearied. As it was, Minx transferred her attention to the dog, and the dog left in a hurry, Minx in hot pursuit.

I had no wish to delay until the mare came back, but it was a minute or so before I could climb to my feet and stay upright. I staggered the quarter of a mile or so to the cabin, feeling near to collapse. Nevertheless, as far as I could judge, apart from my remnant of nose, which was bleeding freely, I had no other serious injuries. Although I felt as if all my ribs were broken, I judged that, at the worst, only a few were cracked.

It was the danger of infection which engaged my thoughts. At best a horse's teeth can hardly be considered sterile, and a mare's habits after having a foal were not calculated to improve matters.

Back at the cabin I bathed my bitten nose. The bleeding was all to the good providing I did not lose too much blood. Lying on the bed, I poured the best part of a bottle of iodine over my nose. A doctor might have thought this rather crude, but it was the best I could do. Then with a good pad of lint and a bandage round my head I lay quiet for a while to think things out.

It was imperative that I should get to Colston as soon as possible. Soon the reaction would set in and I should

be unable to move. Already my nose was recovering from
its numbness and becoming painful. My numerous bruises
and abrasions were stiffening up, and I felt ill.

At the end of fifteen minutes I phoned Pete McLean.
He was out, but his wife answered, and on hearing what
had happened she said she would get in touch with Pete
right away. I said I thought one of the campers would
come in with me, and suggested that it would be wise if
Pete brought the forestry truck as near to the pass as he
could in order to meet me.

I made my way somewhat unsteadily down to the lake,
and the two anglers there were only too willing to help.
They saddled Paint and turned Barney loose, but he insisted on coming along, anyway. One of them brought
his own horse and set off with me for Colston, the other
staying to look after the camp. I was not quite helpless,
and managed to climb on Paint all right.

As we went along the trail I caught sight of Minx feeding peacefully, a foal at her side. Maybe a cougar or a
coyote had made a pass at her offspring, and she had
fought it off, being in the mood to have a go at anything
when I turned up with the pan of oats.

The trip into Colston seemed to be the longest I had
ever made. I was in poor shape and in quite a mess, the
motion of the horse starting my nose bleeding again. I
don't remember going over the pass at all, though I was
still conscious. Pete McLean was at the bottom of the
pass, having coaxed the truck farther up than any vehicle
had been before. He had a mattress in it, and the Colston
doctor was soon at work on me, pumping me full of anti-
tetanus and morphia. He said I'd better get to hospital
right away, and that involved an eighty miles journey to
Calford. I remember little about the trip, but the examination revealed, as I had expected, that the only serious
damage was confined to my nose. I had a few bent ribs,
several highly coloured bruises and some scratches, but
in a few days I was feeling fine. There was no infection,
and I was none the worse apart from my lack of nose.

To me it looked repulsive, and I felt rather self-conscious about it. I was glad to have it covered up, but I could not conceal it for ever.

The Forest Superintendent came to see me and put my mind at rest about my job. He told me that the Ranger in the adjoining district was looking after my area as well as his own until I got back. One district was a full-time job, and it was impossible to look after two. Fortunately, the fire hazard was not serious and the trails had been cleared. He also said that enquiries were being made about my disfigurement. New York, however, appeared to be the nearest place where I could get the necessary treatment, plastic surgery still being in its infancy. He assured me the Department would foot the bill, but I was not at all happy at being the cause of so much expense, and I had visions of being away for a long time and someone else being given my job.

After about a week in hospital, my doctor came to the bedside with a colleague.

"This is Doc MacAdam," he said. "He would like to have a look at your nose."

He peered at it from all possible points, then scratched his head.

"Anything being done about this?" he asked.

He was tall and gaunt and had large hands, and certainly did not look like Calford's leading surgeon. Yet that was who he was. On being told the position he said:

"Look here! I reckon to be pretty good at skin and bone grafts. I use a new method, and though I haven't done any building up of features, I think I could provide you with a new nose. It won't cost you or anyone else a cent. If you don't like it when I've finished I can remove it, and you'll be none the worse. In fact, it would look much tidier than it does now. What do you say?"

He had a hearty laugh, and I immediately took a fancy to this unusual character, whose appearance and manner fascinated me.

"It's O.K. by me," I said.

"Good," MacAdam grinned. Then he turned to his

companion. "You get on to the Forestry Department and see what they have to say about it," he said.

While he was gone, MacAdam told me his theory of how he intended to tackle the job, much of which was Greek to me.

"Now look," he said. "You're getting around all right, and it's only fair you should see something of how I work. I'm doing an appendix and a kidney this morning, and I'd like you to come along. Very interesting if you've not seen it before."

He gave me an encouraging and hefty slap on the back and grinned all over his face.

"I don't think I need see you operate," I told him. "I'm quite confident of your skill."

"Why, I believe you're scared," he laughed.

The other doctor returned at that point to say that the Forestry Superintendent thought I ought to be able to do as I liked with my own nose.

"That's settled, then," said MacAdam, and off he went.

"He's a queer guy in some ways," my doctor said. "He's good and he knows it, and he's tickled to death at having the chance of trying out his methods on a proper piece of work."

"He's asked me to look in on a couple of operations," I said.

"Then do," was the reply. "Come along to the theatre about ten. I'll be there as I do the anaesthetics for him. He'll be disappointed if you don't turn up."

I could hardly refuse, and I duly turned up and was shown to a seat in the "gallery" where there were several students. A large mirror at an angle gave an excellent view of the operating table.

MacAdam came in dressed for the occasion, said "Good morning, fellers," and winked at me. He looked round at his assistants and went on, "If you're all set bring on the subject."

The patient, a woman, was to have her appendix removed, and the moment she was brought in MacAdam's manner changed. He was positively charming, talking soothingly to her until the anaesthetist signalled it was time to start.

"Note the time," said the surgeon, looking at the gallery. "The quicker the job the less the shock."

There followed some quick, deft cuts with the scalpel, exactly deep enough. There was a great deal of amazingly skilful manipulation with a forest of instruments, nurses handing him things and taking them away. All the time he kept up a running commentary, interspersed with funny and very witty wisecracks. As he finished he gave his work a light pat with a gloved hand.

"Fifteen minutes flat," he said. "I've done better."

There was a great deal of the showman in MacAdam. After a short pause for washing up and changing of attire, the kidney patient was brought in, this time a man. It proved to be a longer and more serious job than the appendix, but the commentary was kept up just the same, although there were less wisecracks. I remember the offending kidney was placed on a dish like a head on a charger and MacAdam said:

"Let 'em see it. An excellent example of a rotten kidney."

I was impressed by MacAdam's unerring and, to me, almost magical skill, and I had no qualms as to what might happen to my nose. That afternoon he came to see me.

"I'll do your conk in the morning," he said. "Now tell me, what was it like before? Got a photo?"

I said it was a very ordinary organ, perhaps a shade too long, and produced a snap for him.

"Humph!" MacAdam grunted. "About the same as before, but a little shorter? That suit you?"

He then examined various parts of my anatomy for a suitable spot from which to remove the spare part, deciding upon the upper arm.

"We won't bother about the bone," he said. "It's mostly gristle, anyway. It's the shape that's important."

The necessary preparations completed, the next morning I was wheeled into the theatre. There was no

audience, perhaps because MacAdam was not certain that
he could carry out what was to him a novel piece of work
with his usual aplomb.

I woke up in bed to find a couple of nurses holding my
hands. Evidently they were taking no chances of me
touching my nose, or rather the scaffolding that covered
it. When I was asleep there was always someone hovering
around, keeping an eye on me. MacAdam was a frequent
visitor, anxious to know that my nose felt quite comfortable.

After a few days he said he'd have a look at it, and for
once he looked rather apprehensive as the coverings were
removed. I was watching his expression and was relieved
when he grinned broadly.

" Nurse, fetch a mirror," he said. When it was produced
he added, " Now, have a look, but take no notice of the
hardware."

What I saw was a new, rather pink nose surrounded
by an assortment of pegs and wires, but I could see that
it was going to be all right.

MacAdam was delighted.

" Give it another week and we can remove the hay-
wire," he said, and he went off grinning hugely.

Thus I received a new nose. I had to keep it covered
for some time, and was warned not to allow the sun to
get at it too suddenly. Unfortunately, I found it a
nuisance having a cover flapping about my face on hot
days when I returned to my job, and I neglected the precaution. In consequence, I had my nose sunburnt, which
slightly marred the perfection of MacAdam's work. But
the defects were barely noticeable. A few scars, not visible
at first, made their presence known, and that was all.
Initially, however, the nose was so perfect that MacAdam,
much to my embarrassment, took me almost by the hand
all round the hospital, showing off his work to his col-
leagues. I duly returned to the Ranger Station at Colston
and after her enforced rest and plentiful pasture, Paint
was full of life, and promptly bucked me off when I
jumped on her back to ride back to the barns.

I had not seen the last of MacAdam, however, for although he lived so near to them, he had never been to the mountains. What I told him about them so whetted his appetite that he decided to spend a few days with me at Wind Lake. He was very fond of fishing, but being a very busy man and rarely taking time off, he found little opportunity to indulge his hobby.

In order to relieve him of all trouble regarding supplies and camping equipment, I arranged with a guide in Colston to loan him a horse and bring him out to the cabin. He lived with me, spending most of the time while I was away on patrol fishing in the well-stocked waters.

He thoroughly enjoyed his short vacation, and washing dishes and cutting wood seemed to add to his fun. Mac, as he insisted I must call him, was cutting wood on his last evening at the cabin, and as he was doing an expert job, I remarked on the fact.

" I'm pretty used to any sort of tools," he said, " as well as those of my trade. You must see some of the furniture I've made when you're in town some time."

" Then you've not always been a surgeon?" I said.

" Good heavens, no," he replied. " The first twenty years of my working life I was a carpenter, and a darned good one, too, though I say it myself. Maybe that has some bearing on the way I use the more delicate tools of my present profession. But I don't noise the fact abroad that I've been a carpenter, as it might cause some consternation among the customers."

We laughed at his sally.

" Always, though," he said, " I wanted to be a doctor. I suppose everybody feels like that at some time or other, but with me the longing persisted, almost amounting to an obsession. Back home in the Old Country my father was a carpenter. He couldn't afford to keep me at school beyond the leaving age, much less pay for me to train for a profession, so I was apprenticed to a joiner. I didn't dislike the work and I did well at it, but always at the back of my mind persisted my desire to be a doctor. From the library I obtained all the books available on anatomy and therapeutics, and by the time my apprenticeship to carpentry was finished, my knowledge of general medicine was quite equal to my knowledge of carpentry.

" There seemed to be little future for one of my trade at home in those days, so I packed up and came out here. I soon had a job and earned good money, and that enabled me to buy books to improve my general education. I saved enough money to start a joinery shop of my own, prospered and hired some help and started to make money in a much bigger way.

" I married, bought a house and became a solid citizen, but I wasn't satisfied. At forty years of age I did something which made most of the folk who knew me think I'd gone out of my mind. I sold my business, gave my wife a sum of money and invested the rest so that she was assured of some security. Then, with a small amount of cash, I went to Montreal determined to achieve my lifelong ambition.

" Fortunately I'd warned my wife before we were married as to what might happen, so there was no trouble on that score. Still, I felt a bit mean leaving her to look after the family without my help. In spite of my age, my many years of study made much of what I had to learn dead easy and I qualified in record time. Then came a couple of years in a hospital in the States where I specialised in surgery. That over, I moved back to Calford, sold my house and bought one in another part of the town and put up my plate.

" Except for a few intimates the carpenter was forgotten. At first it was tough going. Then G.P.s started calling me in for operations, and I got the experience and practice I needed. Soon I had all the work I could handle, and it's been that way ever since. I'm over sixty now, but I'm good for another ten or fifteen years yet, especially if I come up here for a week or two every summer. Anyway, I'm satisfied. Maybe the carpentry business would by this time be just as rewarding financially, but I could never get the same kick out of it."

Mac had attracted me from the first, and after hearing

ST11

his story of remarkable courage and determination my
admiration for him knew no bounds. And he was always
one of the most welcome visitors to Wind Lake. When he
passed on, a year or two ago, he must have been some
ninety years of age.

I caught Minx soon after I got back, and neither then
nor later did she show any sign of being vicious. I packed
her and took her on trips, her colt running close behind.
So she must have been in a completely unreasonable state
of mind when she attacked me, and, in the most literal
sense, caused me to lose face.

X: THE MYSTERY OF THE TREE

LATER THAT SUMMER, I had an experience which bordered
on the fantastic. Perhaps I had not fully recovered from
Minx's attack on me, and perhaps the heat, which had
never before affected me, made me see things in a way
I had never seen them while in the Rockies.

On a ridge not far from the cabin at Wind Lake grew
an old Jack Pine. It must have stood there looking down
on the valley longer than any other living thing. It was on
the far side of the lake, well up the slope of a mountain
in a spot maybe where no human foot had ever had cause
to tread. Exposed to the full force of every winter
blizzard, it was also open to every wind that blew.

It was not a tall tree, being perhaps only thirty feet
high, but it was larger in girth than any other in the
valley, its huge spreading branches all leaning away from
the prevailing wind. Even the one or two which had
started on the north side of the trunk were twisted round
it, so that they pointed south, away from the direction
of the worst storms.

On the north side it could be seen that many branches
had begun to grow, but they had been broken off, leaving
simply a knob where they had healed over. The whole
tree leaned slightly to the south; it had often attracted

my attention growing there alone high up on a rocky ridge where no other tree could find a footing, but being on the far side of the lake, I had never been close to it. It was a Sunday morning and I was out in the boat and decided to have a closer look at this old man of the woods.

The climb was well worth while. The tree must have been at least five hundred years old, and there must have been a stern struggle for survival in its early years. Its trunk preserved its size right to the top where it was gnarled like a great clenched hand. It had sent up many new shoots, but none had survived long enough to grow to any height. The velocity of the wind was at its worst, apparently, at the crown of the tree, and no new growth could maintain itself against the winter onslaught.

I was driven to speculating on the tree's remarkable age. No other tree in the valley was much more than a centenarian, but here was one with five hundred years to its credit, and it had not flourished in the most advantageous spot.

At its base huge roots lay on the surface of the rock before disappearing down some crevice. This was most noticeable on the windward side, where three such roots took the strain of the weight of the branches and withstood the tremendous thrust of the wind. Beneath the tree several inches of peaty soil had formed, being a mixture of pine needles and eroded rock, all the cracks and crevices around being filled with it. In time other trees would take root and maybe in another five hundred years there would be several, and the rocky ridge would become covered with soil.

I sat in the shade of the ancient Jack Pine and had my lunch. There was a fine view of the lake and valley, and it might well have been that I was the first human ever to rest beneath the wind swept branches. It was on the opposite side of the lake from the main trail, and very probably the view was just as it had been when the first shoot of the tree thrust its way to the light.

Yet was the view the same? For one thing, almost all the trees in the valley were spruce. I could not see another pine. Had there been many pines at one time? If so, where were their offspring?

There being no great fire hazard just then, and having no urgent duties, I relaxed, allowed my thoughts free play, and found myself reconstructing the tree's history.

Some years before Columbus set sail for the New World, a pack rat or maybe a rock rabbit carried a pine cone up the ridge to the hole in which it lived. Scared by an enemy perhaps it dropped it. A wind carried it into a depression where it remained, perhaps for weeks, perhaps for years. Then along came a sheep or goat, picked it up and chewed it. Not finding the cone to its liking, the animal ejected it, at the same time releasing the seeds it contained. These were scattered over the rock, to be washed away by the next fall of rain, some being washed into deep cracks, where they may remain to this day.

Other seeds found their way into the lichen and one found a resting place in a tiny crack into which had been washed some of the droppings of the animal which had found the cone unappetising. Jack Pine seeds not only need moisture to swell them, but also a lot of heat to germinate them. Often thousands of young pines grow among the dead poles of a spruce forest. This happens after a fire, which has not been severe enough to destroy the soil, and which has warmed it enough to start growth in seeds which have lain dormant for no one knows how long. In any case, I have seen them so thick in what was a spruce forest after a fire, that it can only be assumed that the seeds had remained there since the time when pines had previously grown in the region.

The heat of the rock in which the seed of the Jack Pine nestled became considerable under the hot spring sunshine, causing several of the seeds to germinate. But the moisture quickly dried up and all the seeds lying among the lichen shrivelled and died. Only the solitary seed in the shallow crack made any headway, its tiny yellow shoot turning green at the top as it pushed through the shallow covering of dust.

It was supported by a slender white root which probed

deep into the crack as it pursued the receding moisture. The sun rode higher and higher as summer advanced. There was no rain for months, and the green shoot almost stopped growing. That first summer it hardly reached above the level of the rock, but the root progressed several feet down and sent out feathery side shoots that clung to the damp rock and collected whatever nutriment was available to them.

A hair-like tracery of finer roots felt their way out beneath the lichen, drawing their moisture from the main tap root and feeding on the film of soil made by generations of dead lichen which lay beneath the living. It was hard going in those early days, and probably ten years elapsed before the Jack Pine looked like a tree. Even then it was only a foot or so high, but it was beginning to present a surface upon which the wind could get a grip. The first gale nearly tore it away from its roots.

Other roots thrust out near the surface, some forcing their way beneath thin strata of rock until they came to a crack large enough for them to go down. In time, as these became stouter, they burst through the rock, and these are the same roots which today can be seen straggling over the rock. Meantime the tree was attaining sizeable dimensions. Try as it would, however, it never succeeded in keeping a branch pointing to the north. They were all either broken off entirely or cracked and bent, being forced to point to the south.

The first root continued down and still farther down, following every crack and cranny, often finding itself in a cul-de-sac and having to make another start with a new shoot. But eventually it reached the level of the lake where there was plenty of water. Other side shoots grew out far below the tree where other trees grew, finding their way near to the surface where they were able to help themselves to the more plentiful supply of nourishment to be found there.

When the tree became large enough to produce appreciable shade, deer were attracted to it. They lay beneath its branches in the summer, often all day, away from the flies which pestered them in the valley's lower reaches. Sometimes an elk enjoyed the shade of the Jack Pine, sometimes mountain sheep, and from time to time the bark was trimmed by a bear which came to sharpen up its claws. All these creatures added to the tree's source of nourishment, and it flourished.

It became a solitary sentinel overlooking all others of its kind far below. In another hundred years it reached up to a considerable height, but an exceptionally severe blizzard broke it off near the top. This break developed into a large lump. Again and again it tried to send up a new top, but always, as soon as the new growth was such that the wind could get sufficient purchase on it, it was torn away.

Abandoning the struggle, its nourishment went to the task of increasing the girth of both its trunk and branches. The ever enlarging roots became stout enough to support their now immense burden. Seeds were shed, but never a one took root, at least not in the immediate vicinity of the tree.

Bitter winters and glorious summers followed each other in an endless and violently contrasting procession. During the summers, the tree, its branches spread to the life-giving sun, had all its needs supplied. The lake beneath mirrored it in its clear, rarely disturbed waters. Majestic eagles rested in its branches, pausing between fishing expeditions, or alighting to eat their catch there. The deer and elk used it, not only for shade, but as a satisfactory means for rubbing the velvet from their antlers as the need arose.

For half its life, and perhaps more, the tree's surroundings remained but little changed, except that high summer and deep winter brought their seasonal contrasts. In winter, packs of timber wolves pursued hapless moose or elk, floundering through the deep snow. Let their prey weary, and the wolves did not run in vain. But if the moose or elk could maintain their run long enough, then the wolves were outdistanced and were left to howl in their hunger in the white forest.

Sometimes, in summer, red men came and camped beside the lake, but never on the side where the tree stood. They remained on the far side, where the main game trail wound its way. In those days they came without horses, and they paid their visits but very infrequently, perhaps once in several years. In recent years, however, not only the red man, but the white man, too, were often on the trail in the hot summer months, and both came with horses. The trail, now cleared and made straighter in places, was substantially the same one the game had used when the tree first took root.

Then came an exceptionally dry summer, the kind which happened even less than once a century. The main root of the tree had to work harder than ever supplying the Jack Pine with the necessary moisture. Months passed without bringing so much as a drop of rain, and so dry was the atmosphere that even dew was not produced during the night.

This fierce and protracted dry spell was broken by a thunderstorm of unprecedented violence. But even then no rain came. A tree was struck by a vivid streak of lightning on the far side of the valley, and it flared up like a torch, the fire swiftly spreading. Soon a hundred trees were flaming, and over the forest hung a huge pall of smoke.

And then the rain came. A deluge, it caused the flames to die down. The smoke cleared, being replaced by steam which looked like an ordinary mist. The rain stopped, and then the sun returned, as hot as ever. Within a couple of days the blackened patch where the fire had been began to smoke again, and at night a few flames flickered in the darkness. Another hot day or two, and the fire began to spread again. The larger it became the faster it travelled until the whole of the opposite side of the valley had been transformed into a charred and blackened wilderness. Somewhere at the head of the valley the flames found their way across, and started moving down in the direction of the tree.

Under the urging of the wind the flames were beneath

the tree within a couple of days. The fire rushed up the
hill to the very edge of the forest, and its hot breath
scorched many of the needles on the tree's branches. But
the Jack Pine did not catch alight and the greatest danger
in which the tree had ever stood passed.

Of the millions of trees which had clothed the valley
the pine was the only one to survive, nor had it escaped
the effects of the holocaust. During the years immediately
following some of its branches died, and ultimately they
fell off. All the animals had either been destroyed or had
fled before the encroaching flames, and none was
attracted to the stark wastelands. The birds, too, dis-
dained it, and only the fish in the lake remained, breaking its crystal surface as they rose for flies and other
insects.

The tree inhabited a dead world. The whole valley had
been reduced to a mass of hideous black poles, bereft of
foliage and branches. Fortunately, before all the peaty
soil had been burnt, the early snows had extinguished the
last traces of fire.

With the passage of time, the burned bark fell away
from the dead trunks leaving them standing, a stark
greyish white which was even more repellent than their
former black. But, eventually, life asserted itself again

in the valley. Green made its appearance among the dead giants in the shape of millions of tiny trees. The birds were the first creatures to return, and they were followed, a few years later, by the animals. But it was nearly a hundred years before the valley again assumed its former splendid appearance. Even then old dead trees still extended their whitened trunks towards the sky, pointing above the new growth like ghostly fingers. And there was a difference, because all the new trees were spruce.

Perhaps if another fire ravaged the valley, without consuming the soil, the new growth would be pine, for that is how it seems to happen. But, of course, when the soil is consumed thousands of years must elapse before conditions become such that a new growth is possible. Even then seed must come from somewhere to begin the new forest.

Not for many years after the fire did men come to the valley. First came the red man, this time with horses, and later white men came, too. Not many at first and only rarely. And then they came frequently, cut a good trail and built a cabin. By this time all traces of the fire had disappeared except for a few rotten, fungi-covered trunks to be seen here and there.

It was at this stage of my meditations on the Jack Pine that something happened. I had an experience which has never occurred to me save on this one occasion. The Indians know a great deal about meditation, and they have often talked to me about it and the results it achieves. Because of this I had from time to time spasmodically, when sitting on the porch in the evening, tried to empty my mind of all thought. This art is practised by some of the Indians, and by it they achieve amazing results. But my efforts were half hearted and achieved nothing, for I allowed something to distract me and thoughts crept in.

Sitting there, under the Jack Pine, however, the scene before me changed. I was fully awake, and the scene faded out and another faded in as if I had been watching a movie.

I saw the valley as it had been hundreds of years ago. The spruce had changed to a lighter green. This was the green of the Jack Pine, and the trees were larger. The tree under which I was sitting shrank to a young tree. The sun had been hot, but I no longer felt it, neither was I aware of the breeze which had been blowing before I sank into my trance-like state.

The cabin was no longer there, and the clearing in which it was sited was a primeval forest of pines. The water in the lake was higher, covering a larger area. Much of the flat ground in front of where the cabin should have been was now all lake, and the shelving bank beneath me, where I had moored the boat, was under water to a depth of at least ten feet. The boat was no longer there.

All this time—though how long my state lasted I do not know—I had a wonderful sense of well-being and exhilaration. Then I became uneasy and agitated, and this, I suppose, broke the spell. My normal surroundings were once more before me, and I was at a loss to account for my peculiar experience. I had not been asleep in the normal sense, nor was I ill. Yet all my attempts to find a reasonable explanation of my " vision " proved unsatisfactory.

The next time I passed by the creek that drained the lake I examined it with more than usual interest. The ford where I crossed it was some way below the actual spot where it left the lake. Here it flowed between two steep banks of rock. The number of large rocks in and near the creek at this point left no doubt that in relatively recent times there had been a rock slide which had dammed the lake. This was borne out by a deep pool where the water had flowed over the dam as a waterfall, digging out a hole beneath it. Such a dam might last for a very long time, but the battering of ice during high water in the course of many, many springs would have gradually broken it up, leaving the large rocks that still remained as evidence. I could see no other explanation for their presence there.

It was obvious that the lake had most certainly been as much as twenty feet higher, and, geologically speaking, in comparatively recent times. No doubt the outlet to the lake was still wearing away, but the erosion would only be measured in terms of a minute fraction of an inch in several years.

I was now convinced that what I had seen had been a "photograph" of the valley as it had been, but how to account for the magical moment is quite beyond me.

Only rarely have I told this story, for it is so obviously one which is open to misunderstanding. But I did relate it to an Indian, and he pronounced on it thus:

"White man he go forward all the time. He forget how to go back. He make road and keep to it and not see what is at its side. He miss very much. You find little bit; you keep trying. It very good. Maybe Indian he have no automobile or thunderbird, but he go places faster than white man and still stop where he is." And he chuckled hugely.

My experience served to persuade me that I had discovered one of the secrets of the Indians which quite mystifies the white man. I have a pretty good idea now how it is that some Indians can tell when and where to fish; what bait to use; when winter will start in earnest, and foretell the onset of a blizzard with an accuracy that is astounding.

XI: THE WINTER OF THE WOODEN SPOONS

I FINISHED my summer job as usual on the 31st of October, but had not been back on my ranch long when I had a letter from the Forestry Superintendent. He wished me to act as a clerk-cum-supervisor of a camp of a hundred and fifty men who were to be found jobs in the Forest Reserve. As far as possible the work was to be of a useful nature, but in any case they were to be kept busy.

There would be a foreman and his assistant, usually called the Straw Boss, and a cook. These three would receive the normal rates for such work. The remainder were to get a dollar a day and their food. I was to get my usual summer pay, and my duties were to take care of things for the Forestry Department. I was to set out and find work and attend to the clerical matters. The job promised to be interesting and so I accepted.

During the winter the city of Calford always had an influx of men who had spent the summer working on ranches, lumber camps and in the mines. Usually these men had saved enough to see them through the winter, but this year, due to the aftermath of the 1929 slump, many more of them were out of work, and most of them had not had the opportunity to put in a full summer in a job. In consequence they were facing the winter either broke or nearly so.

The authorities took the not unreasonable view that so many men in town without cash were almost certain to cause trouble, and had decided to get all the single men out into camps, perhaps seeing this as the cheapest and most satisfactory way out of the difficulty. There were to be ten such camps, and I was in charge of No. 1.

Having fixed up with a cowboy friend to take care of my ranch, I set out, along with the foreman, the Straw Boss and the cook, in one of the trucks which was taking some of the equipment to the reserve. There was not much snow as yet and the trucks managed to reach the camp site without difficulty. This was a sheltered shelf of flat ground beside the river, some five miles inside the reserve and not far from the Ranger Station of Tom Arnold, who had been my boss during my first year with the Forest Service.

Tom Arnold, who had met us at the site, insisted that we should visit his Station for a meal, and as there were eight of us, including the drivers, it must have been a bit of a strain. We returned to the camp where a mountain of stuff was unloaded, and the trucks departed. We got up a couple of tents, one being a fair-sized square job for the foreman, Straw Boss and myself, the other the cook tent which was to serve the cook as his home. We fixed up stoves, gathered some wood and put anything which might suffer from frost in the cook tent. That didn't leave much room for the cook, but by dusk we were all set for the night.

Olaf Svensen, the foreman, was built on Gargantuan proportions. Over six feet in height, he seemed to be about four feet wide. In his forties, he was a Canadian-born Swede who had behind him considerable experience in the handling of tough outfits. He had the fair hair and blue eyes typical of the Swedes, and although he was a terrific worker when he felt he must set an example, or when undertaking such items as setting up camp, his hands were always immaculate, and he took a pride in keeping them that way. When not swathed in winter clothing, a waistcoat was visible, and across it hung a heavy gold watch chain. In one pocket was a watch of such dimensions that it resembled a clock, and in the other a large snuff box, containing what he called "snoose," and which he did not inhale but chewed. He would take the box out, tap the lid as if performing a rite, then scoop out a large quantity of the aromatic contents and tuck it carefully under his lower lip so that it looked like a swelling. After a time he would expectorate forcibly and with amazing accuracy through the open door of the stove.

The Straw Boss was tough and looked it, and to his strength he added silence, never speaking unless it was absolutely necessary. He was shortish, but exceptionally broad, and had black curly hair. He was perhaps rather younger than Olaf, and while he enjoyed the name of Clarence Haggerty, his parentage seemed to be a mixture of Scottish, Irish and Italian. Known as Pat, his silent manner did not prevent him from being good company, and he made quite significant contributions to a conversation with little nods, smiles and expressions of serious mien.

The cook was a nondescript, bald-headed little man who ruled his flunkeys with a rod of iron and cooked marvellously.

Setting up camp was quite a job for the three of us, even though Cooky, when not sorting out his own department, assisted with great gusto. We were checking supplies when Cooky produced three unexpected objects.

"And here," he said, "are three wooden spoons. In all my twenty-five years cooking for every kind of outfit, from cow punchers to lumber camps, this is the first time I've been dished out with wooden spoons. What the hell do I use *them* for? Well, I guess we can remember this winter as the winter of the wooden spoons." And, with a chuckle, he threw the offending implements into a box, where they were found when I checked up in the spring.

We four had camp beds, but not the rest of the gang. They were to make bunks, and use mattresses of spruce boughs from the abundant material which surrounded us. Another truck arrived the following day, bringing the rest of our immediate stores, the commissary, and a letter stating that seventy-five men would arrive the following day and a further seventy-five two days later.

The commissary was my responsibility. The large wooden cupboard was housed in a corner of the tent, and it contained an assortment of clothing, footwear, tobacco, cigarette papers, chewing tobacco, " snoose " and soap, as well as many other articles. It was, in fact, a veritable store. There was a list of the contents and the prices to be charged to the men. The prices, although things were cheap at the time, were below wholesale, and they make astonishing reading today. A good woollen shirt cost only fifty cents, and socks of good quality were down at fifteen cents a pair. The thick, almost felt-like German socks that came up to the knees and fastened with a tasselled cord— an almost indispensable garment for the bush—sold for forty cents, while larger items such as a Mackinaw jacket or windbreaker cost as little as four dollars.

Fortunately the snow kept off, and it was not yet too cold when three trucks arrived with the first consignment of unfortunates. On the whole they were a sorry looking lot. Some were reasonably dressed for the winter, while others were inadequately clad. There were some who looked like scarecrows, one or two having threadbare suits, no overcoats and wearing light shoes. Beneath them were remnants of socks, not suitable for winter anywhere, much less were they equal to the stringent conditions of the bush. There were tall ones, short ones, big ones and little ones, but there was not one who was fat. And all were united in one respect: they all looked hungry.

The cook had ready a mighty meal, and our first task was to get our motley seventy-five fed. For a long time there was almost complete silence in the grub tent. Many of the men were eating the first real meal they had had for some time, and they washed it down, if anything was

needed to wash down food into stomachs that had been
empty too long, with gallons of first-class coffee.

After such a meal, all hands were in a willing and
happy frame of mind. My first job was to catalogue them.
I had a table in the entrance of what came to be known
as the bosses' tent, and took down their names, the type
of work they were most accustomed to, and that was all.
Yet never can more difficulty have been experienced in
obtaining such simple information.

I think every European country was represented. Some
spoke but little English, and some of the names were
quite unpronounceable. One little man with a large beard
said, " Me axe man." Then from beneath his walrus
moustache he spluttered something which I took to be
his name.

" How do you spell it?" I asked.

" Give me pencil, pleece."

I handed him my pencil and he wrote like a small boy
in laborious capitals, his tongue protruding to help him
in his task. The result was astonishing, for he had written,
HRYNCZYNCZN.

" Call me John, pleece," he said apologetically, and I
was only too happy to oblige.

The next was his pal, and he had almost no English at
all. He also came from the Ukraine, or from some neighbouring country. His name was not too difficult and, with
John's help, we overcame it. He elected to be called
Ivan.

While all this was going on Olaf and Pat stood by
assessing the human material with which they had to
work. The few who said they were clerks, or claimed
some similar occupation which, in Olaf's opinion, had no
value in the bush, he pounced on at once.

" You're a flunkey," he said. " Report to the cook."

As soon as the preliminaries were completed, Olaf took
charge and began to organise things. I was astonished at
the speed and accuracy with which he weighed up what
we called this League of Nations. From the tent where
the tools were stored he fetched axes.

" Now, all you lumber jacks," he said, " take an axe. We want poles for bunks."

To others he gave brush hooks and told them to cut spruce boughs. The rest were detailed to bring in the poles and boughs, and to collect and cut firewood.

Only John and Ivan remained, as Olaf had commanded them. His reason he gave to me later. " Those Ruskies who call themselves axemen," he said, " can build a god-dam church with just poles and an axe if you want 'em to."

We showed John and Ivan where the bunks were needed, but they needed little telling. They took in everything at a glance. In the sleeping tents there was room for a row of bunks two high all round, and these, with a great tin stove in the middle would be quite comfortable.

" We get axe no, pleece," said John.

" I hope we have something to suit you," said Olaf.

We took the pair to the tool tent where there were nearly a hundred axes, of both single and double bitted kinds. Olaf winked as Ivan and John painstakingly examined every axe, setting aside a short list of about a dozen. Finally, after a most careful scrutiny of these and weighing their balance, John selected a single and Ivan a double bladed job.

Olaf, not noted for his patience, was quite content to wait while the selection was being made.

" Time given to fellers like that to let 'em choose an axe is never wasted," he said as we turned to our tent.

By this time some poles had been brought in.

" We make good bunks quick, pleece, sir," said John, and off went the unusual pair.

The camp was now a hive of activity. From among the trees came the sound of axes being plied vigorously. Between the trees flunkeys could be seen cleaning vegetables, fetching water and shining pots and pans under the critical eye and raucous, rarely complimentary voice of Cooky.

Almost as quickly as the poles were brought in the bunks went up, John and Ivan earmarking a couple for themselves in what they regarded as the best location. On the second night all the bunks were ready for those in camp and a start had been made on those which would be needed by the second seventy-five. A gang was set to cutting and splitting fuel, and a stock was piled outside all the tents in use, the cook demanding priority.

I discussed with Olaf the real work that was to start as soon as the camp was properly organised. Pat took everything in without volunteering so much as a word. The Department itself had suggested certain jobs, and one of these was to cut fire-guards, each enclosing a square mile of forest. They were to be sixty feet wide, and everything within the cleared strips was to be burned. An old wooden bridge which crossed the river on the way to the Ranger Station was to be replaced with a steel one, and we had the job of making the approaches. These were to be on a better site than the old bridge and, on one side, this entailed cutting a road in a solid cliff. The gang that would undertake this task had a job which would keep them occupied all winter.

Tom Arnold, who knew every inch of the country, came with me to mark out some of the fire-guards. We did this by blazing trees every few yards along what would be the outside of the cleared strips.

Olaf had studied the list of men and sorted them out according to what he intended they should do. There were too many nationalities to split them up into national groups, and he compromised by keeping together those of a similar type. When the second seventy-five arrived they were added to these gangs accordingly, there being plenty of work for odds and ends who did not seem to fit into any other category, keeping the camp clean and supplying it with fuel.

In this second batch we had a misfit in the shape of a Chinaman. He complicated matters by announcing that he was a cook.

" This," said Olaf, " calls for some diplomacy. He is not up to bush work, and if I make him a flunkey he'll sulk and be no good at all. If I send him to the cook tent his
ST12*

presence will offend the cook, and he's the one feller who
must be kept sweet."

That, I agreed, was a matter of the utmost importance.

" Right," said Olaf. " Now you stroll down to the cook
tent on some other business and just drop a gentle hint.
See if this can be settled without me making it an order.
Because, if I do make this an order, it will be carried out,
and if this Chink is a good cook we don't want to waste
him. And I don't want the cook cutting up rough, else
I'll get snorty, too."

It worked out perfectly. I went to the cook tent,
ostensibly on other business, and Cooky opened the way
by saying, " What are the new bunch like?"

" Oh," I said nonchalantly, " about the same as the
others. But there's a Chink says he's a cook among them
and I don't think Olaf quite knows where to put him."

" He doesn't, eh!" Cooky ejaculated. " What the hell!
Doesn't Svensen know that a hundred and fifty-four men
is a lot to handle with a gang of flunkeys taking half my
time telling 'em what to do? You tell Svensen to send him
right down here. I'll keep him busy." Then, as an after-
thought, " If he really can cook, maybe I can lie in on
Sundays while he gets breakfast."

As the Chinaman's status had not been mentioned, that
could be left to Cooky. Happily, it turned out that the
Chink was a good cook, so much so that even Cooky
admitted it. In consequence we were a well fed camp,
but Cooky saw to it that there was never any question as
to who was *the* cook.

Within two days of the arrival of gang No. 2, the camp
had settled down. I saw little of Olaf and Pat during the
day except at meals or when I walked round to see how
the jobs were progressing. It was not long before I had
to send an S.O.S. for more stock for the commissary. In
many cases Olaf insisted that proper clothing was pur-
chased before the men started work. The amount of the
purchases was debited to the individuals on the back of
their pay sheets, some being fitted out in a complete new
rigout for less than the amount of their first month's pay.

A team of horses had been hired from a nearby rancher. They were needed to haul in firewood and to bring in supplies when snow made it impossible for the trucks to reach the camp. As the winter advanced it was often impossible for trucks to complete the trip, although the camps were only on the edge of the reserve. Supplying a camp at Sikanaska, for instance, would have been an impossibility, and all were situated where there was either a road or a passable wagon trail.

The horses needed some shelter, so John and Ivan were asked to make one.

" 'Ow many horse?" asked John.

" Four, I guess," Olaf replied, calculating that there might be a visiting team, or that another team might be needed when the approaches to the bridge were being made.

John and Ivan went to work among the trees some way from camp. The horses were not arriving for a few days, and as we were all busy the Rusky pair worked without oversight.

A few days later they came to the tent.

" Horse barns done," said John. " Next job, pleece."

As Olaf and Pat were out I went to inspect the stable, expecting to see some sort of lean-to windbreak. But what John and Ivan had made was a first-rate stable. It was floored with flattened poles and caulked all round with moss. There was a half door so that the top could be left open in milder weather, and even mangers had been provided. The poles for the mangers had been squared, and they fitted so perfectly that oats could not fall through. The whole was thatched with spruce boughs, all neatly fastened down and the ends trimmed. They had in this case had a few extra tools and some nails to help them, but they told me they could have managed with nothing but their axes had that been necessary.

The barn was just about what Olaf had expected, but even he was surprised. John and Ivan worked so fast that it soon became a problem finding them jobs worthy of their skill. They built a meat house, a store house for those things impervious to frost, latrines, and a covered way between the cook and grub tents. Then they constructed wattle fences around the tents to prevent the weight of the snow pushing in the canvas at the sides, but at the same time kept a permanent wall of snow which provided sufficient insulation to keep in a great deal of warmth and exclude draughts. Had the camp been a permanent one I have no doubt that this pair of " beavers " would have had us all housed in log buildings before the winter was over. When at last there was no more for them to do in this way they were put in charge of the horses and made themselves responsible for the fuel supply.

Amongst such a polyglot collection of males there were some doubtful characters, and as time went on I could see why the authorities had thought it wise not to keep them in town. Though the majority were in their various ways excellent types there was an unwholesome leavening which required some consideration.

They had all volunteered to come to the camps. True, there was little else they could do, as they would have been gaoled as vagrants had they remained in town without means of subsistence. But they agreed to come, and it was part of the bargain that they should stay all winter, for the first two months not leaving the camp at all. After that they were allowed to visit town for a week-end once a month if the weather allowed them to get there.

Partly as an incentive to remain in the camp and partly because most of them had little to come in the way of wages, they were not paid until the end of the second month. When that time came, it was amusing to see the pay arrive in the custody of a couple of armed Mounties, who stood by while I paid out. As it turned out, this apparently melodramatic touch proved to be a wise one.

Soon after pay day I went into town in one of the trucks to take in the pay slips and commissary accounts. The truck was well filled with those who intended spending a week-end in town.

Before leaving, John came to me with two addressed

envelopes, plus forty dollars and fifty cents, savings which had accumulated due to very careful spending. He asked if I would get international money orders, two for twenty dollars each, put one in each letter, and post them for him.

This took some explaining, but at length I was certain that I understood his exact requirements. I noticed the same name, that unpronounceable name which he had spelt so painstakingly for me, at the bottom of each address. Of course, they were upside down, but I wondered if it was not *our* way of addressing that was really the inverted method.

I did this for him, and thereafter each month the same thing happened. Most of his pay was divided into two equal parts and despatched to the same two addresses.

One day, evidently thinking that some explanation was called for, he said to me: "You think funny why two Missis Hrynczynczn, no?"

I had noticed this, but took the two women to be his wife and mother respectively or his wife and some other relative, and John had been very high in my estimation for sending so much of his small pay to his home country. I told him I had never thought it peculiar that he should send to two women of the same name. But John was determined to explain.

"Me have two wife and two family," he said. "Three children each wife. It happen this way. In big war my country go phut. No home, no wife, no children any more. Me think all dead." He shrugged expressively. "So me again marry and have three children. Then first family turn up swoosh, just that way, out of nothings. Me emigrate to this country very quick. Now me keep two family and live alone. No good, yes?"

I agreed that the situation was highly involved.

"One day I think maybe save up money and get family out to Canada," he said, and then shrugged mightily and despairingly. "*But* veesh family? Sir, veesh one? You tell me zat," and off he went, scratching vigorously at his mop of black hair.

I could not help laughing at poor John's situation, for he told his story so comically. Evidently he was equally devoted to both families and felt equally responsible for them. Actually his position, through no fault of his own, was really tragic, and it says much for his character that he did what he did. He told me that fifteen to twenty dollars a month each would keep them going and that when he was in work he could ensure that they wanted for nothing.

The work went on apace. Sometimes a gang of Scandinavians would challenge a gang of Latins as to which could cut and clean up a mile of fire-guard the quickest. It was entertaining to watch the chips fly and often they were so near a dead heat that it was the quality of the clearing up and burning of the cut timber which decided the issue.

At the outset the men were willing workers, being grateful for the good food and comparative comfort they enjoyed. But a change was observable when hunger had been appeased and there were dollars burning holes in certain pockets. Discontent revealed itself, and undesirable elements in human nature, checked by hunger and hardship for a time, asserted themselves.

The first evidence of this came to hand when half a dozen men quit camp and hiked into town a good sixty miles away. Two were brought back by the police, each having been fined ten dollars, which was to be deducted from their pay, the penalty for drunken and disorderly conduct. The rest straggled back, dead broke and looking like wrecks. They had walked all night in the bitter cold, not daring to rest in case they never wakened again.

There was one little man, a Latin of some kind, who was not the sort who excited any liking. There was nothing criminal in his nature, but he was a born sycophant. He tried to curry favour at every opportunity, and although he was discouraged time after time, he still persisted, and we gave him the name of the Creeper.

I had the commissary open for an hour each evening after supper, and he came in on one occasion for some cigarette papers. Olaf was reading, Pat was chewing steadily gazing into space, and the Creeper was our only customer. He looked round furtively and whispered in a tone suggesting conspiracy,

"You should watch that Taffy, Mr Svensen, sir. He's up to no good."

"Oh, is that so?" remarked Olaf, looking up from his book. "Just what does he seem to be up to?"

"I don't know right now, sir," replied the Creeper. "But he's well known to the police, sir, and he acts as if he was up to sump'n."

Creeper was arousing my antagonism, but Olaf did not seem to mind in the least. It was not often Olaf smoked, but when he did he liked a cigar and I had got some specially for him.

"Let's have a couple of cigars," he said, turning to me. Taking them, he offered one to the Creeper. "Have one," he invited.

Creeper took the cigar and was delighted that the fore-man had taken so much notice of him. He grinned in a manner that sickened me.

"Guess I won't let any of them over there know how I got this cigar," he said. "They might think sump'n, eh?"

With his usual poker face, Olaf said, "Any time you have some real news you think I ought to know, you can easily come up here in commissary time when there's no one else about." And he winked solemnly.

As customers could be heard crunching over the snow towards the tent the Creeper pocketed his cigar and was ostentatiously opening his packet of papers as he went out.

"That feller stinks," said Pat when we were alone again.

"Yes," said Olaf. "But there could be trouble in this camp. Most of the fellers are decent, but there's quite a few that ain't. The Creeper might come in useful." Then he added, "Apart from that, I hate his guts."

Olaf returned to his book and Pat lay back on his bed

thinking thoughts he was most unlikely ever to communi-
cate.

It was obvious that Olaf was right. Much as we all
disliked the idea of a traitor amongst the men, it was
advisable to know what was going on in a camp where
there were definitely some peculiar characters. From time
to time the Creeper came along with some harmless bit of
gossip, Olaf receiving it without betraying his feelings.
Occasionally the Creeper received a cigar, though by no
means always. And then we received information concerning a project which might well have cost a dozen or
more lives.

Muller, a German, who did the blasting on the rock
project, reported some dynamite missing. Muller, a holder
of the Iron Cross, worked with a chap who had the
D.C.M., which struck me as ironical.

"As you know, Mr Svensen," said Muller, "I always
count every shot to ensure there are no misfires. Yesterday
I opened a new box of Monobel and only used eight. This
morning there was a whole layer missing. I guess they
took a layer figuring I wouldn't notice. But what the hell
does anyone around here want with dynamite?"

"All right, Muller," said Olaf. "Keep this matter to
yourself and I'll see what I can find out."

Later in the day he took the opportunity to speak
to the Creeper when out of hearing of the others in his
gang.

"Know anyone who'd be interested in stealing dynamite?" Olaf asked.

The Creeper looked sly. "Maybe," he replied.

"Well, keep your eyes open and let me know, soon."
And Olaf walked on.

That same evening Creeper slid into the tent, and eyed
Pat and me uncertainly.

"All right," said Olaf. "If you've something to say,
spill it."

"Well, it's like this, sir," said the Creeper, "if I was
caught telling you this I might be murdered."

"You're quite safe here," Olaf assured him, "but you'd

better appear to have come for something." He turned to me. " Give him a can of tobacco."

The Creeper took the half pound tin of cigarette tobacco and holding it prominently in his hand, said :

" If you've lost some dynamite, sir, you can bet your life it's that Taffy. He's been in the hoosegow for ' soupin cans,' and he knows others in town in the same line. Properly prepared he could get a good price for it. Maybe I'll know more tomorrow."

With that, he turned and hurried away.

" You know," said Olaf, " that feller's so darned scared, I'm sure he hasn't told us all he knows. Guess I'd better watch this Taffy."

It was only a little while later that Taffy himself walked into the tent. He was tall, thin, had a long nose and had fishy eyes, and he claimed to be Welsh. While it is unwise to judge a man by his appearance, this man, I felt, would have to prove himself before I had the least trust in him. Olaf was reading intently and Pat's eyes were closed as if he were lost in the deepest thought.

" Gimme some chewin'," Taffy demanded ungraciously.

Olaf looked up and spat into the stove, missing Taffy by a bare fraction of an inch. When Taffy turned to go, Olaf spat again, this time behind him. This rather pointed gesture caused Taffy to turn as if he meant to say something, but, thinking better of it, he stalked out.

" Nice feller," said Pat, his eyes still closed.

It appeared that Taffy was a bully when he was confident that he was strong enough to dominate his victims, and the Creeper happened to be one of them. In consequence nothing that Taffy did escaped his notice. Because of this he knew that Taffy on more than one occasion had absented himself from the tent at night, being away an hour or more at a time.

It was after midnight that same night and we were all asleep when we were roused by an urgent whisper. I could dimly see the face of the Creeper thrust between the tent flaps.

" Mr Svensen, Mr Svensen, quick!" he said.

"What's wrong?" grunted Olaf.

"That Taffy's gone out fully dressed. He went up the fire-guard to the east carrying a parcel."

"Why the hell didn't you follow him?" Olaf demanded.

"He'd kill me, sir."

And the Creeper was gone.

"You two fellers stay abed," said Olaf. "I'll see what this is all about?"

"Maybe I'd better come, too," said Pat, heaving himself up.

"No, you stay where you are," Olaf insisted. "I can take care of two or three Taffys."

He struggled into his clothes and went out. He was gone some time, and then there was a commotion outside and he came in, dragging Taffy by the scruff of his neck. He dumped his somewhat limp burden on to a box.

"Now," he said. "Have you got any more of that stuff, you mad son of a bitch?"

Taffy said nothing.

"If you have you won't profit by it now and it might kill a lot of fellers."

"Serve the bastards right," Taffy retorted. "And I hope you're one of 'em."

"What goes on?" I asked, while Pat sat up in bed observing proceedings in a thoughtful silence.

"Nip up to Tom Arnold's place," said Olaf, "and phone the police. Tell 'em we've got a madman in camp. I'll tell you all about it later."

So I dressed and set off the three miles or so to the Ranger Station.

A couple of Mounties arrived by car at daylight, and Taffy was soon wearing handcuffs. It was then, when Olaf explained to the police, that I heard the full story.

Evidently he had found Taffy without any difficulty, being helped by the small fire he saw in the bush. Over the fire, Taffy was frying dynamite in a frying-pan. Olaf stood well back for a time, and saw Taffy pour some nitro-glycerin into a bottle. He was about to put a couple more sticks into the pan when Olaf jumped out at him. Taffy showed fight, but the Swede soon put a stop to that.

"Now let's go look at this stuff," said the Corporal. "And see if we can find any more."

The type of dynamite we used was perfectly safe unless it had been lying around for a long time and become crystallised, or if it had been frozen and was thawed out too quickly. But reduced to pure nitro-glycerin it was extremely dangerous and under certain conditions exploded with the slightest cause.

Muller had had some experience of the stuff, having used it to loosen up rock at the bottom of oil wells when oil was near, and we took him along with us.

At the scene of Taffy's operations the fire still smouldered. The pan was there and in it a couple of sticks of dynamite. There were more in a paper parcel, and a bottle was half filled with a liquid which had frozen.

Muller examined the bottle and decided that, as the contents were frozen, it was safe. But he was aghast at the idea of applying heat to what had been some half dozen sticks of dynamite when the operator had no control over his materials. When too much heat is applied fumes are given off which, on contact with a spark, would explode. The method of making "soup" Taffy had used had meant separating the gelatin from the nitro by applying heat. The nitro was then poured off into a bottle. As Muller said, however, the action of pouring the warm nitro into the bottle was exceedingly risky.

The Corporal refused to take the bottle back to town, and Muller disposed of it by tying another stick of dynamite to it and exploding it.

The Corporal questioned Taffy as to whether he had any more "soup," warning him that it would go badly with him if anyone got killed. Though the stuff might be frozen now, there was the danger that it could kill an unsuspecting camper during the summer. But Taffy refused to speak.

We thought Taffy must be crazy when we found a bottle full of nitro under the spruce boughs of his bed. Everyone promptly retired from the tent. Muller said it would be safe to handle providing it was not jolted, and he walked slowly out into the bush with it, receiving a flow of advice as to any obstacle in his path which might cause him to trip.

Standing it down very gently, he said: " There you are, Corporal. Take a crack at it with your gun."

" Not me," the Mountie replied. " I'd have to stand too close. I'll get my rifle and have a shot with that."

Half hidden behind a tree, the Corporal hit the bottle first shot and it went off like a six inch shell. Taffy, it seemed, would have received some twenty-five dollars a bottle for his nitro, knowing the people in town who bought the stuff. A letter found on Taffy signed with a pseudonym provided a clue that led the police to Taffy's associates, and all were sent to prison for long spells.

XII: WHEN SWEDE MEETS SWEDE

THE LARGEST MAN in camp was a Swede and he was known as The Big Swede. Unlike Olaf, he was not Canadian born and his English was not too good. He had been troublesome for some time, and seemed to resent any kind of authority, being particularly insolent when Olaf was around, and making uncomplimentary remarks when he was within hearing.

One day Olaf came in looking angry, which for him was most unusual.

"That Swede sonofabitch and me is goin' to lock horns before long," he said. "He's always on the prod, and it's bad for discipline."

I reminded him that we were entitled to get rid of anyone who caused trouble.

"No, that won't do," said Olaf. "It's my job running camps. I can't have it going around that I fell down on the job because of that great hunk of Swede. You'd be surprised how these things travel. Just imagine what it would be like for me in my next job if it was known I'd allowed him to give me the run around. Anyway, I'm boss of this camp and I intend to stay that way."

I was rather worried about this ill-feeling. I liked Olaf,

and could see his point, but I was afraid that in a fight
with that Big Swede he might get badly hurt.

There had been one or two scraps in camp and they
had not been pretty to see. They were typical of such
a setting, being without rules or limits. A fight between a
couple of lumberjacks had ended when one stamped on
the other's face. As it was winter, he wore shoe pacs
which are comparatively soft, and not the steel caulked
boots normally worn on the job. Nevertheless, the victim
had not been fit for work for several days.

The Big Swede weighed some two hundred and
twenty-five pounds and he was fifteen years younger than
Olaf. Hence my uneasiness about the outcome of a mix-
up between them. I mentioned my misgivings to Pat.

"You just leave it to Olaf," he grinned. "I've seen him
trim back the ears of men just as good as that Swede."

The crisis came one night after supper. We had been
a bit late starting the meal, and a lot of men who had
finished were still sitting around, talking. We had a
separate table and did not linger over the meal. As we
went out Olaf said in a quite pleasant manner:

"Come on, fellers, scram out of here. The flunkeys
want to get cleaned up."

We had reached the opening of the tent when the Big
Swede said in a loud voice: "I sit here as long as I vant.
'At bastard ain't fit to run no camp, anyway. He's
yellow."

Olaf stopped dead.

"O.K.," he muttered through tight lips, "this is it."

He turned back to where the Big Swede was grinning
insolently.

"All right, fellers," said Olaf. "Get these tables out of
the way. I like runnin' a camp peaceable, but this skunk
won't let me."

There was a scramble and tables and forms were soon
stacked around the sides of the big tent, leaving a considerable space in the centre beneath the hanging gasoline lamps. Olaf quickly stripped to the waist, handed me
his clothes, and for the first time I noticed the kind of

build he had. There was no fat on Olaf. He was two hundred and thirty pounds of bone and muscle.

The Big Swede was rather less bulky and had a longer reach. Being younger than Olaf, he seemed to have some very important advantages. The minute or so needed to clear the tent was sufficient for word to spread round the camp that a fight was afoot, and a crowd edged their way in, forming an oval around the tent's perimeter. The men who could not get in without restricting the space in the centre crowded about the entrance.

Olaf stood hands on hips while the Swede, who had handed his clothes to his cronies, buckled his belt.

" You've wanted this for a long time," said Olaf quietly, but loud enough to be heard by all in the almost silent tent. " What are you waiting for?"

Goaded by the remark, the Swede rushed at Olaf like an enraged bull, aiming a terrific blow at his head. What happened then promptly removed from my mind most of my anxiety about Olaf.

He sidestepped as neatly as a featherweight. Sweeping one of his massive legs in an arc scythe fashion he caught the Swede off balance and swept his legs from under him. The Big Swede went down with a crash that shook the ground.

" Give him the boots!" yelled the lumber jacks.

But Olaf stood back while the Swede scrambled to his feet, apparently unshaken. Then, for a full minute, the fight was at close quarters, and some fearful blows were exchanged. The crunch of bone upon bone could be plainly heard above the excited murmur of the crowd. Blood made its appearance on both faces, and angry red contusions showed on their bodies. Then the Swede, thinking he had an opening, brought up his knee viciously, aiming at Olaf's groin.

It seemed that Olaf had been waiting for this. With a lightning move he twisted aside, taking the blow on his thigh. In the same second, while the Big Swede's leg was still raised he caught it beneath the knee. Hugging it tight to him, he butted the Swede hard beneath the chin

ST13

with his bullet head. In almost the same movement he kicked the other leg from beneath him, and helped by a heave on the leg Olaf held, the Swede described a parabola and landed on his head.

"Boots!" yelled the boys. But again Olaf refused.

The Big Swede was certainly shaken, but Olaf, apart from breathing more heavily than usual, seemed quite calm. In fact, catching my eye as the Swede was rising to his feet, he winked at me as well as his battered lids allowed.

The Swede's only chance of a rest was to get into a clinch. This transformed the fight into wrestling that was very much "all-in." They were both down when the Swede tried to get his thumbs into Olaf's eyes. Olaf, who was on top, was trying to tear himself free from his opponent's grip. He raised himself, lifting the Swede with him, and when the Swede's head was about a foot from the ground, Olaf, still gripping his wrists, suddenly forced him back. The Swede's head hit the ground with such a force that it was surprising his neck wasn't broken.

This time he did not leap to his feet, but got up slowly, staggering a little. Olaf sailed in for the "kill," but the fight was by no means over. By some miracle of rapid recuperation, the Swede fought back, and for some time there was reasonably straightforward fighting.

Now and again the combatants surged into the crowd, and it was during one such occasion that Olaf aimed a piledriver that missed the Swede and hit one of the onlookers, who had pushed his face forward to get a better view. This caused some hilarity, and the victim was laid at the back, no one being able to spare the time to attend to him further. It was an hour before he came round.

After this mêlée it was obvious that the end was near. The Swede staggered and swung wildly, often aiming at nothing. Nor could he think clearly enough to hatch up further tricks. Olaf showed plenty of signs of wear, but he was still steady and quick on his feet.

There was another short spell of vicious punching

during another brief and partial recovery on the part of the Swede. After that he stood, swaying slightly, his expression vacant. Olaf pushed his face to one side, and hit him on the jaw with a blow that started from the floor. The Swede was out.

No one moved, and Olaf waited for maybe a minute to ensure that his opponent was indeed finished. He looked round the assembly.

" If there's any more of you fellers want to dispute my right to run this camp," he said, " now is the time while I'm on the job."

There were no takers and Olaf strode out.

Back at the tent after a wash and the application of some ointment and adhesive tape, Olaf asked me to take some stuff along to fix up the Swede.

It was three days before the Swede returned to work, and the first time he saw Olaf he grinned wryly and said : " Mr Svensen, you will haf no more troubles vit me. You very goot foreman."

And the Big Swede proved as good as his word.

Olaf, although pretty stiff for a few days, managed to get around to his various jobs.

" When I'm not man enough to handle little troubles like that," he said, " it's time I retired, or went back to navvying."

Pat, who had said little, delivered himself of some unexpected and priceless information.

" I ain't the man you are, Boss," he said. " And if anything had went wrong I didn't feel I could have taken over. So, just in case, I was ready to help out with this the first time he came close enough."

He held up a steel wedge used for splitting logs wrapped in a sock. Pat had slipped out and got it the moment he knew the fight was on.

" Mind," he added, " that was only if things were going bad for you, Boss, real bad. I've got me discretions."

The winter got well under way. The fire-guards were finished, having joined up with those of the camp to the north of us, and having been taken as far south as it was reasonable to go. Although the bridge gang had enough to keep them occupied, the rest were in need of a job, and I had them clear and burn all the windfalls and dead undergrowth to further reduce the fire hazard. Before the advent of spring the primeval forest for a considerable distance around camp looked like a well kept estate.

We lived in tents under conditions as severe as at the Poles, and this was made possible by the abundance of fuel and the plentiful labour available to obtain it. Only during blizzards did work stop, though hours were reduced when it was very cold. There was always an ample stock of fuel outside each tent, so that it was never necessary for any man to leave the camp precincts when the weather was savage. A roaring red hot stove was kept going in every tent day and night, half a dozen men in three shifts of two each doing nothing else but stoke them up. Even so, when the temperature fell to forty below and worse, the cold close to the canvas wall of the tents could be felt like something solid. On the whole, however, conditions were quite comfortable.

The nearest doctor was sixty miles away, but the life was healthy and we experienced no sickness. Nor did we suffer any serious accident. What doctoring was needed fell to me. We had a very comprehensive first aid kit, and I had read up pretty thoroughly the instructions on the treatment of cuts, burns and fractures. Most of the injuries needed nothing more than a touch of iodine and binding with adhesive tape. One or two called for a couple of stitches, but the only case we had of any moment at all occurred when an inexperienced chap nearly severed his foot with an axe.

The men who brought him to our tent said that he had " bled real bad," and someone had applied a crude tourniquet. This, however, was not only stopping the cut artery from bleeding, but was preventing circulation completely, thus threatening a bad case of frostbite. I loosened the tourniquet and blood spurted from the wound.

I sent a man to phone for a car to come out right away,

and gave the patient a shot of morphia. I was still worried about the cold, for the patient, having lost a lot of blood, was getting chilled. We wrapped him up very thoroughly in blankets and gave him some hot coffee.

I had another look in the book of words, and armed with this additional knowledge, I gave the foot further attention right in front of the stove. I managed to get my thumb on the right spot, and then fixed up a tourniquet that did not strangle the whole limb. Then, with someone using this as a tap, turning it on and off as directed, I managed to find the damaged artery and get a clip on it. The tourniquet was then loosened a little, but left on in case of accident to the clip. Finally, I cleaned the wound and strapped it up lightly.

It was some hours before the car arrived. A gang with shovels had been sent to meet it, but after it had left the main road it became stuck several times. I gave my patient another dose of morphia before he left, and heard later that he recovered without being permanently crippled.

By the time spring was approaching our complement had fallen to a hundred and forty. In addition to Taffy and the fellow who had cut his foot, others had left camp. Reaching town, they had been collected by the police either as vagrants or because they broke the law, and we hoped that all the unreliable characters had been weeded out. But we were proved wrong.

The Creeper had supplied information from time to time, but none of it had been worthy of attention. And then, one day, he arrived more furtively than usual.

" I overheard two fellers talking," he said, naming them. " They said it would be pretty easy one night, at the end of the month, when he "—he jerked a thumb at me— " was alone to grab the money in here and light out. They didn't know I heard them."

" There's never enough money here worth taking," I said.

From the first it had been realised that it would be unwise to keep a substantial amount of cash in the camp.

Thus commissary purchases were booked even when the men had money. But it was inconvenient to book every little item, and I accepted cash for such items as matches, a plug of tobacco and a packet of cigarette papers. In this way I accumulated between fifty or sixty dollars during the month.

There had been odd cases of stealing in camp, and one or two of the thrifty ones had placed their money in my keeping. I had warned them not to mention that I was holding it, but it seemed to have got out, as the Creeper now revealed.

"They think he's about a thousand dollars belonging to some of the fellers," he said.

"All right," said Olaf. "Keep your eyes and ears open. And if anything comes of it I'll make it worth your while. Now scram!"

The moment he was out of hearing Olaf gave expression to his feelings.

"I can't bear the sight of that crawling snake," he said. "Still, we must admit he's been useful, and there might be something in this. How much have you got?"

"Around three hundred dollars," I said. "Plus what's in the commissary."

"To be on the safe side," Olaf suggested, "let me and Pat hold it between us, and you put the commissary cash where it would take a bit of finding. It would also be as well if you were not alone at night unless——"

He stopped speaking abruptly and listened.

"Did I hear someone?" he asked.

The snow was crisp where it was beaten down hard, and unless they made a detour round the back of the tent in the undisturbed snow, no one could approach without being heard. There was someone, but it proved to be only another customer. Olaf, however, did not resume speaking until he had satisfied himself that no one was outside the tent within hearing.

"As I was saying," he went on, our customer being well away, "unless we get some idea when the hold-up is to take place, then we'd be wise to set a trap."

"That might prevent me being taken by surprise," I said.

"That's what I mean," said Olaf. "Pat and me could go out as if going to the cook tent or some place, then double back and come in from the rear. If there's anyone in camp with ideas of stealing it's time they were some place else."

Partly for entertainment and partly in the interests of democracy, it was customary for Olaf and Pat to join the boys in a game of cards in one or other of the tents. Sometimes there was a little party in the cook tent, the cook being partial to a game of poker, the proceedings being rounded off with coffee and a snack. I often joined in, but was alone during the hour the commissary was open.

With the possibility of a hold-up, however, it was decided that I should not be alone, and that the tent should never be left unattended. Ten days passed, nothing taking place, and then we had another visit from the Creeper.

"Them two I told you about," he said, "have been leaving their tent after supper for a night or two. I checked they weren't in any of the other tents. Maybe they was watching points, huh?"

"Maybe," Olaf agreed.

"I've noticed there's been two of you in here all the time, lately," the Creeper smirked. "So maybe they won't get the chance they're looking for."

The Creeper departed and Pat sighed, evidently with relief.

"I guess that feller's practising to be a private eye or summat," he said. "Must spend all his time watching someone. Queer pastime I call it." And he lapsed into his customary silence.

"We'll try out that plan tomorrow," Olaf decided. "And see what happens."

The next night, supper over, Olaf and Pat went off towards the tents, it being too dark for any watcher to see which tent they entered. Pat had left me his sock with

the wedge in it with the exhortation to "Crown 'em at
the first sign of nonsense."

Hearing the crunch of feet I placed myself within easy
reach of the cosh, but my visitors were only legitimate
customers. I resumed my reading, keeping my ears open,
and heard a slight noise behind the tent. I felt by no
means at ease under the circumstances, and was relieved
to hear Olaf whisper, " O.K. It's us."

There were several clients in the next fifty minutes or
so, and it was about time to shut up shop. I had heard no
more of Olaf and Pat, and I was hardly expecting any
further clients as they all knew I kept to closing time
fairly strictly. We had assumed that, if any hold up was
contemplated this was about the time it would take place,
for there was little likelihood of anyone else coming to
the tent.

Our assumption proved correct, although the manner
of the arrival took me by surprise. There was no attempt
at a silent approach. There was the crunch of feet on the
snow, the flap was pulled aside, and the first face I saw
told me that here were the men we were expecting.

I gave no sign that I understood their intentions, but
put down my book and rested my hand on Pat's cosh.
The pair, who had so far given no trouble, would have
arrived quite free of suspicion had it not been for the
Creeper's warning.

They entered the tent, one remaining at the entrance
out of reach. He drew a gun and trained it on my midriff.

" Give us the money quick," he snarled, " and keep
dead quiet."

I had no intention of indulging in heroics, and the gun
had a definitely menacing appearance. They had kept
the weapon well hidden, for the men were not allowed to
have guns while in camp.

" You've drawn a blank, chaps," I said. " There's not
more than five dollars in the place."

" We know better," snapped the one with the gun.
" Come on now, where——"

He never got beyond that. There were quick steps, and

then an avalanche launched itself into the tent in the shape of Olaf, Pat right at his heels. The holder of the gun had no chance. He was half turned to see what was happening when Olaf bowled him down and flung himself on top of him.

This was the moment for me to join in, and I hit the man nearest to me most satisfactorily. He fell back, and Pat, who had jumped over the pair on the floor, caught him.

It was all over in a matter of moments. Olaf rose, the gun in his hand, his man having lost all interest in the matter.

"You're breaking my neck," the other yelled. "I quit."

The police car could not get any nearer than Poker Creek, the little settlement five miles away. Under adequate escort the pair were marched off, to serve what ultimately proved to be a two year stretch in the hoosegow.

In April work became more plentiful. Most of the men we'd had with us had saved up a bit, and the camps were closed, only Olaf, Pat and myself remaining to pack up. There were some large bonfires, and it was rather sad to see all the work of John and Ivan go up in smoke. But

everything had to be cleared before the summer brought the danger of fire.

Then Olaf and Pat left and I was alone, waiting for the trucks to arrive to collect the equipment. During the week or so of waiting I checked all the tools and surplus supplies. All the tents were packed except for the one I had shared with Olaf and Pat all that winter. For the first and only time I came near to feeling lonely in the wilds. What had been a busy camp full of life was suddenly just a pile of boxes, bundles and heaps of ashes.

Then the ice on the river broke. It was not a large river, its rocky course being perhaps three hundred yards across at the widest places, and in summer the water was only a sixth of this width and was shallow enough in parts to be forded on horseback. In winter, when the cold was really intense, the ice became so thick that there was not enough room for the water to flow beneath it. When the temperature rose a little, though it might still be below zero, more water came down. After very cold spells thousands of little springs, which had almost stopped flowing, broke out again and added to the flow. Then the river, blanketed by clouds of vapour, flowed over the top of the ice. The steam rose from chill water, which soon froze again. This continued all the time, and as winter advanced the ice became tremendously thick, filling up the whole of the river's course with a solid block of ice, save for the small space underneath.

This, of course, wore a larger channel as time went on, but with the much warmer days of March it was still unable to take all the extra water, and the process of overflowing continued. In some places the flooding turned to the consistency of treacle, which froze and made a small dam. This grew as freezing water flowed over it until a steep slope was formed. Thus the surface of the ice was by no means flat, but more like great frozen waves. It was good sport skating on these steep slopes and finding banked turns around which it was possible to speed as if on an automobile race track.

This great mass of ice had been splitting with the noise

of gunfire and groaning under the enormous pressure. It had given way at the sides and risen several feet to make way for the water which increased in volume as the days grew warmer. Then a great deal of water roared frothily over its surface as well. After a particularly warm day the ice at last gave up the ghost, and broke up. The noise was indescribable, having a quality all its own.

Huge masses of ice were trying to move down the river. They up-ended to fall with a deafening and nerve-racking crash. They slid over or under each other, and huge slabs weighing many thousands of tons reared on end, being visible above the tree tops.

That night the noise was such that it was almost impossible to sleep, and the ground shook as though from a series of earthquakes. But in the early hours the frost on the higher slopes got a hold and the movement in the river subsided. By morning the flow was only half the volume of the previous day. Masses of ice lay in confusion, some of them having torn great bites out of the bank, tearing out large trees in the process.

I walked for a way down the river. At a bend masses of ice had been forced out of the river and had taken a short cut, carrying with them all the trees and soil, and leaving an enormous iceberg stranded some fifty yards from the original course. It was easy to imagine how, in a great river like the St Lawrence, a whole town had been obliterated in this manner.

As the day wore on it became really hot, and the water rose swiftly. Once more the battle with the ice was resumed. By evening, with the river running at its highest yet, it seemed that most of the ice from higher up had come down. For apart from the stranded lumps, so large some of them that they made little rivulets as they melted, and odd floes which rushed on their way with frequent noisy collisions, the water had a fairly free run. Farther down, in the city, men would be ready with dynamite to break up jams that would endanger the bridges. Massive buttresses had been built to break the ice and to take some of the strain, but under the impact of an unbroken mass of ice they would have been swept away.

The camp was finally cleared and it was almost time for me to take up my summer duties again.

So ended the winter of the wooden spoons. I never came across Olaf, Pat, the Cook, John and Ivan again, but they cannot be forgotten. They had in them some of the strength and rigorous spirit required in the wilds. They were men worth knowing, and they are well worth remembering.

EPILOGUE

WHAT IS THE POSITION in Canada today? This is a question I am often asked by people who seem to imagine that civilisation no longer has a frontier. Behind such a question it is possible to detect the old pioneering spirit and the love of adventure. It is prompted by the desire to break away, if only for a time, from our modern, highly organised way of life.

For those who long for something different, who have a wish to taste excitement and adventure, Canada offers all that they need. But once such a life has been adopted it is almost impossible to relinquish it. I have done fairly well in the way of adventure, starting with one war and finishing with another, and it is only in the last few years that I can claim to have settled down. Yet even now, with what is called late middle age sneaking up on me, my feet still itch to tread new ground, and as I get closer to the time when it will be too late, the itch increases.

For the young, and the not so young, Canada still promises adventure in plenty, and riches too, for those who have the good fortune to find them. And if you chance to miss them, as I missed them, there is still a wealth of highly rewarding experiences.

It is very necessary, however, to know exactly what you want. People go to Canada, exchanging a city job in Britain for a city job out there, and they soon complain that the change has disappointed them. They return home, lamenting that things out there are not the same as at home. But those who desire something exactly like what they have now have no reason to move.

In Canada things are different, and it may not be easy to get the job for which you have been trained. It may well be that your way of doing it doesn't happen to be the way it is done out there. But if you are able to adapt yourself to anything that comes your way, and you are willing to turn your hand to trades other than your own, then Canada is your country.

There you will not be regarded as a foreigner. There is a stretch of territory still unoccupied, and it is nearly as large as the whole of the United States of America. It is all yours, or at least as much of it as you can take.

Canada is larger than the United States, yet only the southern fringe of it is what we think of as civilised. It is true, of course, that civilisation has pushed its way from coast to coast, taking in three thousand miles of territory in the process. But not far to the north is a frontier that has still to be pushed back, and behind that frontier are millions of square miles of almost virgin territory. Even omitting the region above the Arctic Circle, where life is too severe for most, there is still an average of a thousand miles stretching to the north anywhere from Quebec to Alberta, plus a large part of British Columbia, where there is not a road of any kind. No railway threads its way through these immense regions, and there is an almost total absence of population.

There are settlements, such as Great Bear Lake and Slave Lake, which are served by aeroplanes, but they appear as almost invisible pinpricks on a scale map of Canada. Dropped off anywhere en route to these settlements, you would be in country that few white men have ever travelled. In fact, the chances are a hundred to one that you would land where no human foot has trod before. Even the Indians living in this vast land can be counted only in hundreds.

During the war, a road was built from Whitehorse, in the Yukon, to Norman Wells on the Mackenzie River. That road spans five hundred miles and not a town or village can be discovered along its entire length. Anyone leaving it could walk for weeks either way and not meet a soul. Once off the road, walking would be the only possible means of travel.

It is difficult visualising a piece of land as large as Britain with a couple of people in Essex, two or three

more near Carlisle, and a village with a few score inhabi-
tants in the centre. Yet, in Canada, north of 55°, you could
find regions just as thinly populated, and not once, but
many times.

In such a huge land there is plenty of ice and snow in
winter, but the summer is good. And the north, being in
parts at a lower altitude than farther south, has in such
regions a less severe winter. There are minerals which
have barely been touched, and uranium may be amongst
them. There might even be gold awaiting discovery.
Certainly there are furs, and there are millions of acres of
timber. There are still huge areas suitable for ranching,
and they await the men with the wish and will to make
this land their own.

There are the Forest Reserves and Parks to be seen,
where the wild is fairly easy to approach, and done on
foot, and for the person living in Canada such trips can
be cheaper than normal living elsewhere.

An officer acquaintance of mine decided to go to
Canada after the war. His resources were limited to his
gratuity, for he had neither a trade nor experience that
would be likely to help him out there.

At first he worked as a clerk in Montreal, but this prov-
ing too tame, he went west. His next job was driving a
truck in Calgary, Alberta; then he got a job on a ranch
and graduated as a proper cow hand. Now he has a well-
paid job with a surveying party in the wild heart of British
Columbia. That's the way of things in Canada. At times
it may seem tough, but it is worth it.

Come to think of it, that's the whole point about the
country. Canada is well worth while. It is big enough to
absorb you and your desires, no matter how large they
might be. It is big enough to meet all your needs, too. It
has a price, of course, and generally demands it. But it
gives more than it takes. Canada still needs the pioneer,
and it welcomes him, and it rewards him. Not always with
money, but always with things that are really worth
while.